INTRODUCTION

Mary McAdams Clark and Rosa McAdams Campbell beside Big Darby Creek

Of two sisters one is always the watcher, one the dancer.
—Louise Glück

The story of Samantha McAdams and her daughters Rosa McAdams Campbell and Mary McAdams Clark was preserved by Mary's daughter, my great-aunt Florence. She was a collector, an accumulator, or, as my mom would say, a pack rat. At her death she had copious amounts of fine china, trinkets, and baubles. Much of it originated with her parents and grandparents. The real treasures that Florence passed on to her niece Carolyn Clark and nephew Jim Clark were the McAdams family Bible; dozens of Clark and McAdams family pictures; letters written by Samantha and her daughters, Rosa and Mary; and books ranging from the 1850s to the 1960s.

Samantha and Mary lived within a mile of each other in Allen Township, just outside North Lewisburg, Ohio. Rosa lived twenty-five miles away in Richwood, Ohio. The two towns are suburbs of Marysville, in central Ohio. They wrote letters to each other like we use cell phones today. About one hundred of the letters, dated from 1897 to 1920, provide an insight into the life and times of three well-to-do farming families.

The Victorian era was ending. The world was rapidly changing as a result of the industrial revolution, advancements in science, the railway boom, and a new form of communication—the telephone. The women's suffrage movement was in full swing. At the turn of the twentieth century, agriculture was the primary economic engine for fewer than a thousand citizens.

Samantha's hometown of Marysville is the Union County seat. Two papers were published there, representing two political parties. Several lawyers and physicians practiced their arts in the city. The railroad serviced industrial freight and farm commodities. Roads that led into Marysville from outlying communities were improved with gravel and graded. Markets, bakeries, individual shops, and banks serviced the city and surrounding area, including two large department stores owned by Hattie Clark's husband Donald Carmean. There were five churches—Presbyterian, Methodist, Congregational, German Lutheran, and Catholic—that ministered to the diverse immigrants.

Other than special shopping trips to Marysville, Samantha and Mary spent nearly their entire lives in North Lewisburg. The railroad connected North Lewisburg with Urbana and Richwood. The state capital, Columbus, was thirty-five miles by rail from nearby Woodstock. Travel was by horse and

A WINDOW INTO THE PAST

A Window into the Past: a Mother and Two Daughters'

Written by
W. Bruce Matthews III

ISBN: 9798650131571 (paperback)

CHAPTERS

buggy or train. North Lewisburg had a dry goods and general merchandise store, a drug store, and a furniture and carriage factory. Several doctors and a dentist tended to local patients. Mary's cousin Andrew Beltz owned the flour mill. It was a close-knit community, as most residents were related in one way or another and attended one of the three churches: Methodist, Quaker, and Catholic. The town of North Lewisburg, Ohio, lit the streets with electricity in 1897, as the letters between the mother and two daughters began.

Samantha wrote her letters with no punctuation or paragraphs. Mary and Rosa wrote beautiful, well-punctuated letters. All three were good spellers. They wrote as they spoke, which is a little different than the way we speak today. The letters printed in this book are edited slightly for readability without losing the writing style of the author.

The ladies wrote letters about the endless, repetitive, tedious work on their farms. They reported the joys of the changes in styles of hats and dresses. When they came along, the children's major events were news. A new Victrola, washing machine, or stove was always exciting news between the women. Samantha, Mary, and Rosa also wrote of the town gossip, friends getting married, friends becoming ill, and friends passing on. The community did not escape tragedies. The ladies wrote of them.

Their husbands, Wilmer McAdams, Lester Clark, and Isaac Campbell, were described in detail in the letters. The men focused on their agribusinesses and were not particularly emotionally or physically supportive of their women. They tended to the crops and large animals on the Darby Plains. By 1915, Rosa moved in with Wilmer and Samantha, the families had telephones and automobiles, and the letters ceased.

The soils adjacent to Big Darby Creek were rich and productive. They were also wet in the springtime and after heavy rains. The men's work in the fields was weather related. Good-weather years provided plentiful food for the hogs, cattle, horses, and family. While the men were out in the fields, the women raised chickens for eggs and, when they stopped laying, for dinner. Daily they would race to the hen house to beat the rats for the eggs.

Wilmer McAdams and his two sons-in-law, Lester Clark and Isaac Campbell, all about the same age, had varied successes. Wilmer McAdams was conservative and stable and what Samantha desired after a turbulent upbringing. Will, as he was known, was not willing to go into debt; he rented property, including a farm from Lester and Lester's brother Henry. Farm deals came and went.

Lester and Isaac encouraged Wilmer to purchase a Pottersburg farm. When Wilmer didn't do the deal, Lester bought the farm and rented it to Wilmer and Samantha. Late in his life, Wilmer would finally purchase twenty-six acres just outside of North Lewisburg, on the road to Marysville, from Howard Beltz for cash in 1913.

Lester Clark was more successful than the other two men. He had more of a head start, inheriting land and money. Lester was driven. He owned five farms in three counties. He was totally immersed in his land, opportunities of future real estate, the Union County Democratic Party, and his award-winning livestock. He was divorced with a teenage daughter and over twice the age of Mary McAdams when they married. Lester had little time for Mary and, when they came along, his children.

Isaac left Kansas for Union County in 1888 as an experienced yet broken man. He was a founding father of the cattle town Grenola and owned a large farm. After he accidently fired the gun, a series of events happened that culminated in him leaving four children in Kansas. Why he moved to Ohio is unknown, but he had many Kansans looking for him for his debts. After a short courtship, he married seventeen-year-old Rosa McAdams, who was half his age. Isaac and Rosa purchased a farm, but his real interest was in the trading, purchasing, and selling of livestock. Good at turning stock, he quickly accumulated wealth.

The three farmers could afford to hire day laborers when needed. The women would cook meals for the laborers. During threshing season and after morning chores, the meals would take a good part of the day to prepare for so many men. The ladies were able to hire women to help clean house, can, and perform other household duties. Rosa and Mary had dayworkers mostly year-round. Samantha hired help as she needed it but wanted more help than she hired.

Samantha's granddaughter, Florence Clark, also left four informative diaries detailing her everyday life in the years 1925–1929. I wish Florence were still around so I could thank her for the interesting writings. The diaries detail her dress for the day and how and where she was going and with whom. Upon completion of Capital University's school of music, Florence enjoyed her life in the late twenties.

The carefree "roaring twenties" were welcome after eight years of family turmoil. She had many men wooing her, which was fun. She played the piano at the picture show, in a quartet, and at the Methodist church. She was a good singer, speaker, and music teacher. Florence was quite an item around North Lewisburg, until her marriage to the postmaster Lester Overfield.

Of equal importance in saving this snapshot of history is Mary Ann Wesley. Mary Ann, my father's partner for ten years until his death, had a wide background in photography and history. Mary Ann knew the value of the photos and artifacts. She preserved what very well might have been thrown away.

My wife, Julie Matthews, has spent hours and days assisting me in cataloging the photos, letters, and books. The books are interesting and cover a range of subjects from the Civil War to relationship matters. All the books were written and copyrighted between 1845 and 1925.

Julie and I met Virginia Clark Clemens in the North Lewisburg library while we were learning more about my family history, and did we learn! Jinny took Julie and me around North Lewisburg, showing us homes and gravesites and telling us historical family stories. The three of us were standing in North Lewisburg's Broderick Cemetery next to Caleb Clark's tombstone. Jinny looked at me and said, "Look all around you. All this land was owned by your family." Relatives have a common closeness. Cousin Virginia Clark Clemons has continued to be a friend since the day we met.

Without Mary Ann, cousin Jinny, and Julie, the lifestyles of my great-great-grandmother Samantha McAdams and her daughters, Rosa Dell and Mary Florence, would not have been preserved. The letters and diaries capture wry humor, joy, and positive spirits during the mundane, and the faith that helped them endure the hardships and drama of everyday life in a town of a thousand people at the turn of the century. The story is told through the letters and family photos. The journey through the documents is fascinating and leaves many questions unanswered.

Enjoy life on the farm in central Ohio at the turn of the century.

Bruce Matthews

The Ladies and Their Families

Mary Florence McAdams Clark, Samantha Rose Draper
McAdams, and Rosa Dell McAdams Campbell

*The work of today is the history of
tomorrow, and we are its makers.
—Juliette Gordon Low, founder of
the Girl Scouts of America*

Samantha Draper was born July 13, 1847, in Marysville, Ohio. She was the eldest of six children—herself, Julia, John, Flora, James, and Charles—born to Gideon and Chloe Orahood Draper. James Polk, president of the United States, was preoccupied with the Mexican-American War, and Brigham Young had just arrived in Salt Lake City, Utah, with his Mormon pioneers. Others born in 1847 who would go on to change lives of Americans included Thomas Edison, inventor of the light bulb; Alexander Graham Bell, inventor of the telephone and metal detector; outlaw Jesse James; and women's suffrage pioneer Anna Howard Shaw.

Chloe Draper was a godly woman of Presbyterian background. Her children, the center of her life, were schooled in religion and academics. Samantha grew up to be a religious person like her mother and sixth great-grandfather James Draper. A man of strict piety, he was then known as "James the Puritan." James emigrated with his wife, Mary, in 1647 from Yorkshire, England, to Roxbury, Massachusetts, to set up a clothing business. He came from a long line of clothiers. The name *Draper* literally means "maker and seller of woolen cloth." James owned several looms that clothed the early settlers of the colonies. His clothing business was a three-hundred-year success, producing textiles in New Hope, Massachusetts, until 1967 as the Draper corporation. James also was a soldier in the colonies' first war, the King Philips War, which took place in Massachusetts against the Wampanoag in 1675.

In 1785, President Thomas Jefferson and Congress declared they would grant unclaimed lands in the Northwest Territory as payment or back pay to veterans of the American Indian Wars, Revolutionary War, and War of 1812 for the benefit of the US Treasury. States gave up their claims to lands in what now are Alabama, Michigan, Minnesota, Wisconsin, Mississippi, Illinois, Indiana, and Ohio for future settlement. Samantha's great-grandfather Gideon Draper was a Virginia veteran. He secured a Revolutionary War land warrant as a reward for his service in the Revolutionary War. The Virginia Military Reserve was bordered by the Ohio, Scioto, and Miami Rivers. The Reserve included Champaign and Union Counties and Big Darby Creek.

Virginia Military Reserve
(source: virginiamilitary.org)

Like many other early pioneers of the Virginia Military Reserve, Gideon Draper, a widower, moved with his son Ira and Ira's family to Taylor Township, Union County, Ohio, in 1836. The family carved a small farm out of the woods on their newly acquired land grant.

Ira's son, also named Gideon, married Chloe Orahood of Paris Township in 1846. Chloe's grandfather Amos Orahood, also a Virginian, came to the Darby Plains seeking to chisel out a farm on grant land before 1815. Gideon's occupation was as a day laborer working for farmers and merchants as an "extra hand" around the Marysville area, doing jobs like clearing trees and stumps, cutting sod, threshing wheat, and cutting and shelling corn.

In the mid-1800s there was no immunity and few medical remedies against diseases such as tuberculosis, smallpox, measles, chicken pox, cholera, whooping cough, and influenza. A cholera epidemic swept through Ohio in 1849. Samantha's brother John and sister Julia both succumbed to illnesses and passed away before 1860.

After years of political differences, the Civil War began April 12, 1861, when Confederates under Gen. Pierre Beauregard opened fire upon Fort Sumter in Charleston, South Carolina. Three days later, President Lincoln issued a proclamation calling for seventy-five thousand militiamen. Recruiters quickly filled the call.

Robert E. Lee, former superintendent of West Point and son of a Revolutionary War hero, was offered command of the Union army, which he declined. Virginia seceded from the Union on April 17, followed by Arkansas, Tennessee, and North Carolina, thus forming an eleven-state Confederacy with a population of nine million, including nearly four million slaves. The Union had twenty-one states and a population of over twenty million.

In May of 1861, Gideon Draper signed on to Company F of the Thirteenth Regiment of the Ohio Volunteer Infantry (OVI). He was summarily discharged two and one-half months later for shooting one of his own troops. In the spring of 1862, Gideon volunteered and entered the Civil War a second time. That fall Samantha's mother, Chloe, and sister, Julia, suddenly took ill and passed away. Samantha was fifteen years old. Samantha and her brother Charles went to live with the Marshall family in Marysville. Sister, Flora and brother, James, moved to Salem, Ohio, to a distant Draper family and worked a farm.

Gideon's second call to war unveiled a second occupation. The Civil War Draft Registration recorded Gideon's new occupation as a preacher. His actions were far from ecclesiastical. Gideon was a private in Company F of the OVI Seventeenth Regiment led by Lancaster, Ohio, native Gen. William Tecumseh Sherman. Gideon was with Sherman on the March to the Sea. He was in the midst of bloody battles as heavy casualties were taken to his unit as they made their way to Atlanta from May to September 1864.

Gen. Sherman and the Union army's commander, Lt. Gen. Ulysses S. Grant, believed that the Civil War would come to an end only if the Confederacy's strategic capacity for warfare was decisively broken. Sherman planned an operation: scorched earth warfare, or total war. Although his formal orders specified control over destruction of infrastructure in areas in which his army was unmolested by guerrilla activity, he recognized that supplying an army through liberal foraging would have a destructive effect on the morale of the civilian population it encountered in its sweep through the state.

Sherman's armies reduced their need for traditional supply lines by living off the land. Foragers, known as *bummers*, provided food seized from local farms for the army while they destroyed the railroads and the manufacturing and agricultural infrastructure of Georgia. Sherman's orders were direct, and soldiers of Gideon's personality and life skills thrived on the orders.

Sherman's field order of November 9, 1864, included the following instructive. The army was to forage liberally by not entering buildings but gathering provisions from gardens and orchards. They were to destroy cotton gins, mills, bridges, and roadhouses only when met by hostility and freely appropriate mules and horses to replace the regiment's jaded animals. Able-bodied slaves who could be of service could be taken along, especially if they were able to bear arms.

Gideon was already good at pillaging for food and supplies. Prior to the march from Atlanta to Savannah, an imbedded reporter for the *Marysville Tribune* wrote about how the campaign was going while resting outside of Atlanta. Private Gideon Draper was specifically mentioned as the "terror of Billey" for his talents, which he would utilize for a lifetime. Billey was Gen. William Sherman.

Correspondence of the *Marysville Tribune*
Letter from the 66th
Near Atlanta, Ga.
August 5, 1864

Editor Tribune: -Again I am permitted to write you a few lines which I hope may provide interesting to some, if not all, of your readers.

Sherman's army are now holding a well-fortified position in front of the "Gate City" and ere many days you will hear of the capture of the city, and it I mistake not, a great portion if not all of Johnson's army. Our Cavalry under Gen. Stoneman have succeeded in cutting the rail road, and Atlanta is now in a state of siege. From what we can learn from deserters and prisoners the rebel army is greatly demoralized.

In conversation with a prisoner who was taken on the 1st inst., I was more fully convinced of the importance of the coming Presidential election. He admitted that if Lincoln was elected there was no hope for the Southern Confederacy; but said, "If the Peace men elect their candidate they would still hope on." This fact the soldiers have been aware of for some time, and I feel safe in saying that Lincoln-Johnson will receive a tremendous majority of the soldier's votes. Let the Loyal men of the North stand firm to the work at home, and I assure them the soldiers will do their duty on the field and at the ballot-box.

I visited the 18th Ohio Veteran Volunteers yesterday, and found Sgt. Dougherty in fine health and spirits. The Regiment is greatly reduced since the campaign. They now muster only ninety-three men.

Gid Draper, "the terror of Billey," is doing well. Heavy fighting has just commenced on the extreme right. Report says the right wing is advancing. If so, we have no fear of the result as it is commanded by Gen. Howard, who since the death of Gen. McPherson, has been in command of the 125th, 16th, and 17th Corps. The loss of Geary's Div., 20th A. C., on the 20th invt., is as follows:

Candy's Brigade,	70
Jones's Brigade,	157
Ireland's Brigade,	280
Aggregate	457

The Division was repeatedly charged upon by Hood's Corps but they were as often repulsed with heavy loss. Gen. Williams is in command of the Corps. Hooker being ordered to Washington where we hope he will receive a commission of more importance than one corps. As briefness is my object, I remain yours,

Very respectfully, H. J. L.

Gideon was quite a character and plagued by his own torments. He became familiar with the bottle, a good tussle, and Marysville law enforcement. He was a good story for the Marysville newspaper reporters. Articles about him were written until his death in 1898 and beyond. If one was from Marysville and did not know Gideon or know of him, they were new to the area.

Gideon did not go home to the children after the war. The children were scattered and no longer saw or heard from each other. There is no mention of any brothers or sisters by Samantha in her letters. There is no mention of her father, Gideon, even though he resided within twelve miles of her in Marysville for decades and was very well known. During the war Gideon was admired for his toughness and bumming. Back home in Marysville, his skills and habits were not always appreciated. For the next thirty years, Gideon lived a troubled, listless life. The Marysville newspapers covered some of the antics of this colorful character through the years.

The following was printed in the *Marysville Tribune* newspaper May 5, 1869:

A difficulty occurred on Sunday week ago, between Gid Draper and Nelson Guy on one part, and Joe Starr on the other, at or near a disreputable house a mile or two southwest of town, in which Draper is charged with an attempt to shoot Starr. Draper was arrested, and the Court still being in session, a special Grand Jury was summoned to examine the case. They found a bill for assault and shooting. As the case could not be got ready for trial at this term, Draper in default of giving bail was placed in prison, where he will remain until the September term, unless a special court will be called to dispose of the case.

Gideon made the news again on October 14, 1878. The *Marysville Tribune* reported:

A shooting affray occurred near Marysville, Ohio, Saturday morning. Gideon Draper shot James Hall with a shotgun, the shot taking effect in the back part of the head and arm. Cause: Whiskey and two soiled doves. Draper was arrested by Marshal Bonnett, but made good his escape and is still at liberty.

Gideon was a good storyteller, and people were more than eager to hear his stories. The following June 18, 1879, article from the *Marysville Tribune* exposed his guileful imagination utilized for his advantage.

Got the Best of Him

B. Myre is said to be a descendant of the Hebrew persuasion, and runs a shop on East Center Street for the disposition of liquors—wholesale and retail. A good story is on the fly, regarding a bit of transaction since the last term of court. Gideon Draper, whose personage is known to almost everyone in the county—old and young alike—and as pretty generally understood, has an appetite for this class of traffic, which at times grows considerably beyond his power to quench, unless it is done with the vile fluid above mentioned. Some time since, Gideon, being without the proper root to satisfy his appetite with this article, concocted a plan, which worked well to his advantage. He proceeded to the above liquor establishment and had the proprietor to draw him a half pint of his best. The proprietor of course was glad to comply and measured out the liquor into a bottle and Gid took it and stored it safely away in his inside coat pocket, and proceeded to entertain the Hebrew, with words relating to business and matters of general interest. He seemingly forgot the liquor he had purchased and started out, when a thought struck him, and turning around, said "O, I nearly forgot to pay you," and as he was reaching in his pocket for the money he farther said, "Now my friend, this is a set-up job on you. I was sent here to buy this liquor of you by Prosecutor Woodburn, in order to catch you, but I don't want to be mean, and will give it back to you, and warn you to beware." After saying this seriously, he reached in his pocket and returned to the trafficker a bottle and then went out. When the proprietor went to return the liquor to the barrel, he had occasion to smell it, we presume to see if it reached the standard. To his utter discomfiture he held in his hands a bottle filled with cider. Gideon had brought the cider with him, and in returning the bottle, gave him the cider instead of the liquor. A plan well laid and adroitly carried into effect.

Gideon lived adjacent the Mill Pond, not far from the courthouse. The February 10, 1881, article from the *Marysville Tribune* documented another of Gideon's tribulations.

A continuous rain of forty-eight hours has melted the snow, so that Millcreek has attained an unprecedented height, and with floating ice is tearing away fences, trees and bridges. The floors of Gideon Draper are covered by a strong current, and the house is only kept in place by being moored to trees with ropes.

If the *Marysville Tribune* needed a good story, all they had to do was look for Gideon. Below is an article from February 16, 1884:

A Feat with Brains in It

Gid Draper tells a story, and solemnly vouches, for the truth of it, that will bear repeating in a newspaper. He has a small frame cabin standing on the banks of Millcreek, near the upper bridge, which he calls his citadel, where none dare molest him or make him afraid. Last Wednesday Millcreek rose to flood height, and in the evening the waters surrounded the cabin and all the circumjacent territory. The outlook was decidedly threatening, as well as magnificently grand and imposing. Gid has a few chickens and one gander, which constitute his entire interest in livestock. The chickens were in a coop, and among them was an old hen, the reputed mother of said gander, she having hatched two goslings last spring one of which subsequently died, and the other was the hero of this narrative. The waters were encroaching rapidly, and Gid waded out and rescued the chickens, all but old hen, which for some reason was left to take care of herself. He retired to bed during the evening, supposing the waters were at their height. About ten o'clock he heard the gander at the door chattering as though he had something important to communicate. On getting up and opening the door the gander swam off in the water in the direction of the chicken coop, and the door was closed, Gid supposing the bird to be somewhat aquatic in his habits, could take care of itself in that sea of waters. It was not long till Mr. Gander made his second appearance at the door crying lustily for admittance. Gid once more got up and opened the door, and to his astonishment there was the old mother hen snugly seated upon the gander's back! They were admitted into the house and assigned to dry quarters. The old hen no doubt often deplored the strange habits of her erring child; but on this occasion she seemed to be thankful that she had raised a son who was a good swimmer, and who upon an emergency like this could provide for her safety. The chicken coop washed away during the night. It is supposed that before it started the hen flew out and lit upon the gander which was plying about the coop, whereupon he piloted her to the house. If anyone can beat this little narrative of animal affection and seeming wisdom, we will patiently wait for it.

Late in life Gideon seemed to have an awakening. The *Marysville Tribune* reported the following on September 28, 1892:

Hon. Gideon Draper of Hardin Co., made his annual visit to this, his old home, during fair week. Gideon, some time ago, received the grant of a pension of $12 per month, with over $900 back pay. He informed us that he had not touched liquor of any kind for the past fifteen months, and he says he will stand to that resolution.

Six years later, Gideon died a pauper at the age of seventy-one in the Soldiers/Sailors Home in Sandusky, Ohio.

***

Samantha Draper married Wilmer McAdams of Allen Center on November 8, 1868. The youngest of five children, Wilmer grew up nearby on Josiah and Mary Ann McAdams's farm. He and his siblings, Henry, Nancy, Missouri, and Alpheus, were close through their lifetimes. When they married, Samantha was twenty-one years old, and Wilmer was nineteen.

Samantha Draper

Of the McAdams siblings, Wilmer was the only one to continue the farming tradition. Wilmer and Samantha rented the farm adjacent his father's farm. Renting a farm could be on a cash basis or, more often, that of cash and a share of crops, and Wilmer and Samantha were sharecroppers.

In the era when three of ten children died before five years old, diseases such as scarlet fever, whooping cough, and cholera were prevalent and devastating. Samantha and Wilmer had their traumas. Their first son, French, was born in the summer of 1869 and died the spring of 1871. Rosa Dell was born two months later. Another son, Willie, was born in 1873 and lived for four days. Mary Florence was born September 11, 1875.

The loss of both sons was tough on Samantha, because of the separation issues of her own childhood. Samantha put all she had into child-rearing. Rosa and Mary grew up in a close-knit, religious home. Samantha made sure that the children were well schooled. Wilmer tended the large animals and crops, while Samantha and the girls took care of the fowl, small animals, garden, canning, butchering, butter making, and housekeeping.

During Rosa and Mary's childhood, the industrialization of the United States was following the period of reconstruction after the Civil War. New rail lines connected major cities with factories for moving the raw materials of the rural countryside. Cost of production was going down, and speed of manufacturing goods and equipment was going up.

Benjamin Goodrich opened a rubber plant in Akron. Rutherford B. Hayes from nearby Delaware, Ohio, was elected president in 1876. James Ritty of Dayton created the cash register. Thomas Edison invented the electric light bulb, transmission lines, and the phonograph. Alexander Graham Bell worked on development of the telephone.

The women's suffrage movement was in full swing. Susan B. Anthony, Clara Barton, and Anna H. Shaw joined forces and traveled the countryside, preaching the value of women in society and women's independence and decision-making, and empowering those who sought work outside their home.

The main roads between North Lewisburg and Urbana and Marysville were being ditched and graveled. Bicycles with two wheels the same size were invented. The combination of the technical advancement of the roads and the improved mode of transportation proved to be very freeing for the rural population.

For the Victorian lady, the dress of the day required much fabric. The lady of leisure and taste required not comfort but elegance. Corsets, loops, bustles, and layers of petticoats created shape and style. Puffed-sleeve blouses and dresses as well as the ankle-length skirt left the freedom of the bicycle to the boys and young men.

In 1888, seventeen-year-old Rosa Dell McAdams met Isaac Newton Campbell, eighteen years her senior. A quick summer romance ensued. On November 12, 1888, Wilmer McAdams signed the marriage license, allowing his daughter Rosa to marry a man more than twice her age, thirty-five-year-old Isaac.

Isaac Campbell was born in 1853 in Kane County, Illinois. During the late 1860s, Jesse James and his gang were robbing banks owned by postwar Republicans throughout the Midwest. James's illicit activity was received by many as a continuation of the Civil War. Confederate sympathizers mistakenly saw the James gang, who fought for the South, as taking the bounty from the rich and keeping it for the poor. Isaac's family immigrated to the uncivilized land of marauders, Elk County, Kansas, in 1868. They staked out a farm in the Indian territory of south-central Kansas.

At the age of twenty-eight, Isaac married sixteen-year-old Elise Walworth. They had three daughters and a son together. Soon he owned 720 acres of land; 340 acres of it was cultivated. The farm had fifteen acres of orchard, three good houses, a barn, and plenty of running water. The entire property was fenced. Isaac extensively engaged in stock-raising. He had 142 head of cattle and many hogs. He bought and shipped livestock. He was known as one of the best stockmen and a genial gentleman and was popular in the county.

The Kansas City, Lawrence, and Southern Kansas Railroad, routed through Elk County, was completed in 1879. Isaac and several others built a new town, Grenola, beside the tracks. It soon became a rowdy cow town. Within four years Isaac Campbell was a wealthy man. Life was good for the swank rancher. That was until the April evening of 1885, when the gun discharged.

Newspapers of south Kansas from Wichita to Pittsburg carried the news:

A fatal and distressing accident occurred Monday last eight miles southwest of Moline. Mr. Isaac Campbell, a prominent citizen and wealthy farmer of Greenfield township, while handling a revolver in the house accidentally shot his wife, the ball passing through the abdomen. He and Mrs. Campbell had been handling the weapon, and both supposed it was not loaded. Mrs. Campbell died the next morning.

A drought hit Kansas in 1885, which severely affected crop yield. It was costly to feed the animals, and Isaac sold the stock he had as quickly as he could for what he could get. The mortgage banks called in his loans. A year later the Grenola newspaper reporter wrote, "I.N. Campbell left Thursday evening for Sedalia, Missouri, where he has recently engaged in the mercantile business with J.T. Smith." Leaving his four children with his brother and his wife in 1887, he moved to Union County, Ohio, with little to show for his past life.

Isaac and Rosa Campbell (back right) with Isaac's children, 1889

Isaac and Rosa began their life together on a small farm near Richwood, in northern Union County, and rarely visited Isaac's children in Kansas. Ike, as he was known, enjoyed buying and selling. He spent much of his time traveling and trading livestock. Ike and Rosa's years together were not always joyous. Ike suffered from frequent, severe headaches and at times temperamental violence. The twenty-seven-year union produced no offspring.

Rosa Dell Campbell

Seven years after Rosa married Ike, Mary Florence McAdams also fell in love with an older man with a child. On September 11, 1895, nineteen-year-old Mary wed forty-eight-year-old Lester W. Clark. Lester's daughter, Hattie, twelve years old at the time, was not too thrilled with her new stepmom.

Lester's father, Caleb Clark, was born in Harpers Ferry, West Virginia, on July 4, 1814. As a child, Caleb immigrated to Allen Township, just east of North Lewisburg, with his parents, Angus and Elizabeth (Green) Clark.

Nehemiah Green, a Quaker and Elizabeth's father, was a provisioner during the Revolutionary War. A privateer, he owned a ship and ran supplies for the colonies. British Gen. William Howe's naval blockade of Philadelphia was effective. Howe's navy captured Nehemiah Green and transported him to Southampton, England, as a prisoner of war. While detained in Forton Prison, he was poisoned. He recovered and remained there until the end of the war.

Nehemiah earned a Virginia Military grant of land just outside of North Lewisburg for his service. Angus and Elizabeth emigrated west with him. They worked on the farm, and "Nehemiah kept a one-story log house known as the Blackhorse Hotel" (*North Lewisburg Gazette*, September 29, 1876).

Angus Clark acquired wealth and a vast amount of property around North Lewisburg during his lifetime. He died in 1859, at the age of seventy-six. His wife, Elizabeth Green Clark, lived until March 20, 1881, reaching the age of ninety-one.

Angus bequeathed $500 to each of his daughters, Rebecca Clark Critchfield, Catherine Clark Snuffin, and Elizabeth Clark Shaffer. Angus's land and the remaining cash were split among his three sons, Caleb, Nehemiah, and Shepherd.

In 1841, twenty-nine-year-old Caleb Clark married thirty-one-year-old Rachel Beltz. Rachel was originally from Bedford County, Pennsylvania. She arrived in North Lewisburg with three of her brothers, Philip, Andrew, and Daniel. Caleb soon purchased one hundred acres of land in Allen Township, adding to his inheritance. He and Rachel settled the property east of North Lewisburg. He kept adding to his first purchase until he owned 580 acres in Allen Township.

Politically, Caleb was strongly Democratic and was the recognized leader of his party in Allen township for many years. He served as his township treasurer for six years and also filled various other local offices. The ten years before the Civil War, the four years during the war, and the ten years after were turbulent times, to say the least. Antislavery Unionist Republicans gained popularity in the more urban areas leading up to the war. Also known as Radical Republicans, their goal was to abolish slavery. President Lincoln, elected in 1860, held a more moderate view on slavery. Conservative Union segregationists were Democrats as well as proslavery successionists.

Although North Lewisburg was not a stop on the Underground Railroad, the Friends Church supported local ardent abolitionists who helped runaway slaves with their reach for freedom. Thomas Winder, a farmer north of town, would harbor escaped fugitive slaves. Caleb's Quaker grandfather, Nehemiah, would have approved of Winder's actions. Much of Caleb's politics were intertwined with the stark dichotomy of beliefs in the small community.

A man of enterprise, Caleb was known for breeding and rearing fine horses and assisting in the construction around Allen Township and North Lewisburg. He died in 1869, leaving his daughters, Susan Clark Caryl and Ellen Clark Shaffer, $12,000 each. Caleb's land was split equally between his sons, Angus, Lester, and Henry. They also received $12,000 apiece. Rachel died at home six years later.

Lester Clark farmed 136 acres of his father's old homestead at the junction of Inskeep-Cratty Road and the Erie Railroad with his first wife, Jerusha Poling Clark, from the time they were married in 1870. Lester continued to acquire prime farmland in Logan, Champaign, and Union Counties. He raised award-winning draft horses and was annually recognized at the county fair. A strong Democrat, Lester was a permanent member of the Union County Democratic Committee. In 1885 he was on the ticket for Union County treasurer.

Jerusha divorced Lester in February 1884 and received a judgment of custody of their daughter, Hattie May, and one hundred dollars every three months for support. Jerusha died one month later after a short illness. Lester wed Mary Florence McAdams eighteen months later.

Hattie May and Lester Clark

Lester and Mary Clark, 1896

Letters from the Turn of the Century

North Lewisburg, Ohio, circa 1905

*The average farmer's wife is one of the most
patient and overlooked women of the time.*
—The American Farmer, 1884

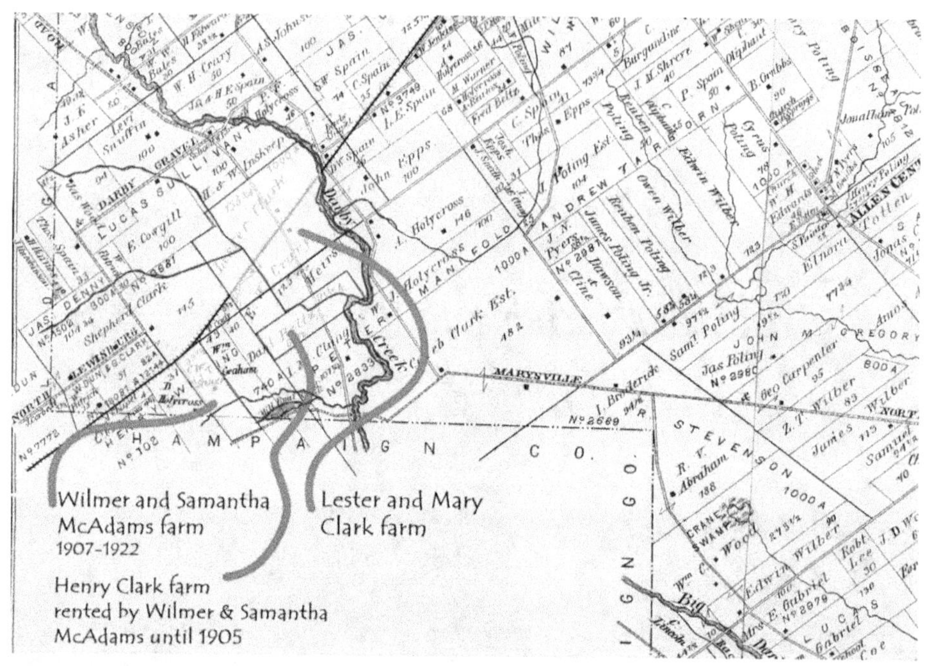

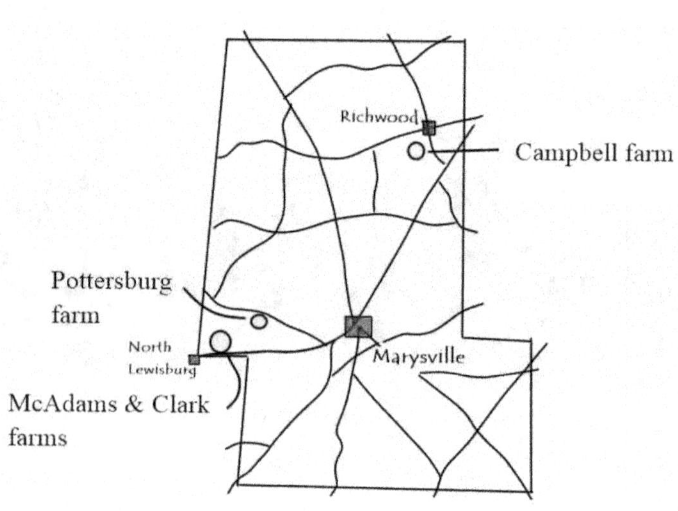

Union County Ohio

North Lewisburg is situated in northeast Champaign County, Ohio. Immediately north is Logan County, and west is Union County. Spain Creek flows through town to the east into Big Darby Creek. The land around the town was fertile along Big Darby Creek. Agriculture was the way of life. The town of nine hundred people had a grist mill, hardware and general merchandise stores, and Quaker, Catholic, and Methodist churches.

By 1850, the Erie railroad connected Cincinnati, one hundred miles southwest, to the industrial cities of Cleveland and beyond. The railroad cut through the small town and Lester Clark's property one and a half miles from the town center. The rails connected North Lewisburg to Urbana thirteen miles west and to Richwood twenty-four miles northeast. Columbus, home of the state fair, where Ohio's best farmers go to admire, buy, and sell prize livestock, is thirty-five miles southeast.

Despite the growth of industry and urban centers, America was still predominately rural. Seven out of ten people lived on farms or in towns of 2,500 or fewer people. Many residents were related to each other. The third and fourth generations of the McAdams and Clark families were related to the third and fourth generations of the Beltzs, Caryls, Spains, Snuffins, Polings, Barnetts, and Orahoods. The adjacent communities of Woodstock, Milford Center, and Allen Center were dotted with the farms of the cousins.

Outwardly the women had a central yet passive role in the family and business. They were the keepers of their households and the guardians of moral purity for the family. Children were nurtured. The husbands were encouraged in the difficult and physical demands of their farm tasks.

During the late 1800s, social activist Susan B. Anthony formed the Equal Rights Association, starting the women's suffrage movement, which lasted until 1920 with passage of the Nineteenth Amendment. She was pilloried for working to destroy the institution of marriage. Clara Barton, founder of America's Red Cross, struck up a friendship with Susan B. Anthony after a stint as a nurse in the Civil War.

They traveled the country campaigning for women's rights and equality. Anthony and Barton preached temperance as a women's rights issue. Laws at the time gave husbands complete control of the family and finances. A woman with a drunken husband had little legal recourse even if his alcoholism left the family destitute. If she obtained a divorce, which was difficult to do, he would easily end up with guardianship of the children.

Women were standing up against society's wrongs. They were beginning to chafe against what historians have called the "cult of true womanhood" or the "cult of domesticity," an ideology developed during the early nineteenth century that tied a woman's virtue to piety, submissiveness, and domesticity. The only "true" woman was a pious, submissive wife and mother concerned exclusively with home and family.

Harriet Beecher Stowe was a prolific author and staunch women's advocate. She was one of the first editors of *Hearth and Home* magazine, one of many publications appealing to women. Stowe campaigned for the expansion of married women's rights to own property and women's rights to acquire money and inheritance.

Anna H. Shaw, the same age as Samantha Draper, was one of the first ordained female ministers of the Methodist Church. She traveled to churches preaching women's rights as well as the gospel. She would later become a physician and spend her lifetime as a political activist.

Reform groups were proliferating across the United States. Women played a prominent role in temperance leagues, religious movements, and moral-reform societies. Rosa and Mary were part of the suffrage movement. They were members of the Methodist Church–sponsored Epworth League. The purpose of the association was to encourage and cultivate Christ-centered character in young adults through community building, missions, and spiritual growth.

Literature of the period set high standards for moral rectitude, cleanliness, and cheerfulness. Harriet Beecher Stowe and her sister, Catherine Beecher, wrote *The New Housekeeper's Manual*, over six hundred pages to assist in training young women for the distinctive duties that would inevitably come upon them in household life. The manual covered philosophy and practical methods in depth to teach young women the skills that needed to be mastered so they could be an independent, self-reliant success. Subjects included health and child-rearing, efficient home and kitchen design, firing the stove and washing clothes, and canning and cooking.

Montgomery Ward published a small mail-order catalog known as "the wish book" in 1874. Ward delivered a "satisfaction guaranteed or your money back" purchase to the rail stop of a woman's choice. Soon the company offered a 240-page catalog that had over ten thousand items to keep women abreast of the latest conveniences, fashion, machinery, and lifestyles of the day.

Social reformists, societies and women's leagues, newspapers, books, and catalogs contributed to a new way of thinking about what it meant to be a woman and a citizen of the United States.

Samantha, Rosa, and Mary, like all wives of farmers, were vital partners in their husbands' businesses. They each kept a clean, neat, pious home and filled it with the smells of roasted chicken, sweet jams, and fruit pies. They also had charge of the kitchen garden and chores of feeding and butchering chickens, small animal husbandry, churning butter, and making sausage. They sold eggs, butter, and milk. They sewed clothes and darned socks. The women were mentally and physically strong and interested in local and world events.

In 1897, former Ohio governor William McKinley was one year into his presidency. C. W. Post had stolen Dr. Kellogg's Maple Nut cereal formula and started mass-producing it as Grape-Nuts. Richard Sears printed his first catalog to give Ward's catalog serious competition in the mail-order business. The town of North Lewisburg had been recently lit with electricity.

Rosa and Ike Campbell lived on their farm in Richwood, a train stop away from Mary and Lester Clark's farm on Inskeep-Cratty Road, just east of North Lewisburg. Samantha and Wilmer McAdams resided on their farm rented from Lester's brother, Henry Clark, near Mary and Lester's farm.

Samantha was close to her daughters, Rosa and Mary. The women wrote frequent letters of joy, anguish, and events of everyday life. The letters shine a light on their lives on their farms of Union County, Ohio.

Mother, Home And Heaven.

Many a time a cheerful home and happy faces do more to make good men and women than all the learning and eloquence that can be used. It has been said that the sweetest words in our language are "Mother, Home and Heaven," and one might almost say the word home includes them all, for who can think of home without remembering the gentle mother who sanctified it by her presence. And is not home the the dearest name in heaven? We think of the better land as the home where brightness will never end in night. Oh, then, may our homes on earth be the centers of all our joys; may they be as green spots in the desert to which we can retire when weary of the cares and perplexities of life, and drink the clear water of love, which we know to be sincere and always unfailing.—Ex.

This newspaper clipping was in a letter from Samantha McAdams.

An April 11, 1897, letter from Rosa to her mother, Samantha, and sister, Mary, read:

Dear Parents and Sister:

…I have had the neuralgia over my right eye for the days since we moved. We cleaned the worst of the dirt upstairs Friday. It was covered with cobwebs and wasp nests. Ike has had an old man helping him cut down trees a day and a half. They cut down four. He got some gate posts and cut the rest into wood…and has taken out over twenty stumps…I baked a pan of biscuits and they weren't fit to eat so I dumped the rest out to the chickens and baked again…

My hens do pretty well. I got 4 ½ dozen eggs this week. The cows are gaining in their milk. I have made 22 pounds of butter. There is a peddler that comes by every Wednesday. He pays 12 cents [a pound] for butter, half cash. He gives 7 cents for [a dozen] eggs…The butter is as yellow as gold…The kittens get all the game they want. The place is just alive with rats and mice. We put arsenic upstairs. We have them about cleaned out of the house…

I remain your loving daughter and sister,
Rosa Campbell

P.S. I forgot to tell you about one of our neighbors. Mr. Cheney hung himself…I guess his mind was affected. He was well off. He owned 600 acres of land and was respected by everybody.

The November 28, 1897, letter from Rosa to Samantha and Mary:

Dear Parents and Sister:

I must tell you we have seven young hogs; they were a Thanksgiving present…We have a new wagon. Ike took the butter to Marion a week ago and got 17 cents per pound…Ike hasn't husked much corn yet. Ike went to Marion again. He got 20 cents [a pound] for three pounds of butter to one man, 15 cents for 5 ½ pounds at a store and the balance for 14 cents. Ma, if you soak your dried corn overnight and put it on top of the stove and cook it a little, it will be better than to cook for so long…

Your affectionate daughter and sister,
Rosa Campbell

P.S. You had better come for Christmas.

On February 8, 1898, Rosa wrote a letter to Mary:

Dear Sister:

I received your welcome letter and was glad to hear from some of you after so long…Our work hand was here most of last week and the week before. Ike and him sawed down trees most of the time. My chickens are doing pretty well. I get over 3 dozen eggs a week. They are worth 12 cents. We have been going to church…We did not get to go Sunday. Ike had the worst spell in his head he ever had. The pain went all over his head, mostly in the back of his head…hoping to hear from you soon.

I remain your loving sister,
Rosa Campbell

The following is the March 17, 1898, letter from Samantha to Rosa:

Dear Children I will write you a few lines…Will has cleaned the garden and made a new grape arbor if you were here you could have a couple of grape roots. My onions are coming up but I have them too close together I want to sow some early lettuce seed and cabbage seed. Will put in a day yesterday looking for a horse but they didn't find any of them to suit. Henry bought some calves of young Snuffin. He thinks Will and he can make money feeding sheep. He wants your Pa to cut the grass this summer. He will furnish two hands and your Pa one hand. It gives [Will] one fourth. What a fine time I will have cooking for work hands…I am going to fry some cakes write soon.

From your mother
S R McAdams

After a visit to Richwood, Mary wrote the March 22, 1898, letter to Rosa:

Dear Sister:

I just got home after waiting at the depot for over two hours. My geese are laying. My ducks hadn't laid any since I was at your house until this morning…If you come out soon enough, bring me a root of syringa and honeysuckle as mine are just about dead. The rats took all of the eggs from two old hens I set in the barn. I have 11 little chicks now. It has rained so much Darby is just booming. The water is nay up in our cellar. Must close and wash my dinner dishes. Lester is going to town so I had to write in a hurry. Write or come out soon.

Your sister,
Mary

Samantha replied to a letter from Rosa on April 10, 1898, exclaiming the news of flood damage following a torrential spring rain.

Dear Children we got your letter yesterday eve…Mary expected you for dinner we were there for dinner. She cooked thirty eggs and had a chicken cooked. She has 20 little chicks. I have 2 hens hatching and two more set. We have five sows and 14 pigs. The sows eat the first one's pigs. The red sow only had three and some of them are missing…

We had the worst flood that has ever been here the water was up in the yard Sunday morning. On Tuesday it was up over the pike…it came up to the second step at Mary's kitchen. Lester was out till midnight taking care of the lambs. One of his sows drowned. The water was so deep he couldn't cross the road. It was up in his crib and washed Mary's hen's nest out of the shed…It made a clean sweep of the Beltz boys' fences. It would pay to come and see some of the ruin. It broke through the dike in several places…People have come from miles to see the wreck. It took the bridge between here and Lester's. I sell about 16 dozen eggs a week…The old cow brought 30 dollars and 30 cents…The old cow had a farewell race before she died. They didn't kill her the first shot. [It] hit near one of her eyes. She got out on the road. Will got on the mare and took after her when she got up to Lester's she broke through the wire fence and run to the woods. They got her out and she started up the road and [ran] as far as Loudon's. They got her turned into a lot and killed her there…We are to have a new iron bridge over Darby [Creek].

S R McAdams

The May 16, 1898, letter from Samantha to Rosa followed another flood a month later.

Dear Children…Well we had another flood, on small order…Will went out and gathered the hail up in his hands. It looked like chunks of ice. You ought to be here to catch fish the men say there are lots of large ones. Across the road the water was too high to catch them…The cows run in the road…Something has taken 32 of my little chickens I had 51…Did I tell you Will bought Lute's mare? He paid 80 dollars…come or write soon.

From your mother
S R McAdams

The following is the June 16, 1898, letter from Mary to Rosa:

Dear Sister:

Received your epistle and was glad to hear from you. Well, Lester did not come home Saturday noon. [He] did not come until Saturday night.

The trial was not until Saturday. Haven't heard yet how it came out. Effie Caryl [Lester's cousin] and Lula Spain were here and stayed all that night. Mrs. Critchfield [Lester's cousin] and her daughter Mrs. Fisher and her little girl from Mansfield were here the next Wednesday for dinner.

I went to Marysville on Friday and run onto Addie and he came out with me and stayed until Sunday…I have 287 little chickens now. I notice the smallest ones are beginning to look droopy. My old chickens have the cholera worse this summer than they ever had it. Addie said he was still thinking of making you a visit. Your hired hand was here Tuesday. I did not know him until he said he worked for you. The weeds are getting a start in the garden. We had young chicken and new peas for dinner Sunday.

Most of the girls around here are getting something or other wrong with them from riding their wheels [bicycles] so much. I'll have rice pudding for dinner. You had better come over…We got more rain than we needed. It looks like it will rain in a day or so again. My lame chicken that you laughed at so much is walking alright now. Write soon.

Your sister, Mary

Henry, Merle, and Aerie Spain Clark
circa 1898

Many farmers rented their farms. Larger landowners would take payment in cash, crops, or both. Henry Clark, Lester's brother, rented to Wilmer and Samantha McAdams. In a July 24, 1898, letter to Rosa, Samantha wrote:

Dear Children your welcome letter came to hand Thursday night. We were glad to hear from you. We are through harvesting we threshed Friday we have 177 bushels of wheat our share. Ira Burris threshed some today. He had 500 bushels. Henry gets two-thirds. Lester hasn't threshed yet. I don't know if he has all his hay up yet you ought to see the stalks of fine hay we have here…We had about 80 tons altogether the old meadow gets better every year…we have not got any bridge yet…Howard Beltz and Miss Graham were married Thursday night. I have neuralgia in my head and have been so lame I could hardly walk. Mary had 400 chickens. The rats are taking them. I guess a weasel killed one the other night. Bit them through the head. I wish you were here for me. I would let you cook.

From your mother
S R McAdams

The following is the November 28, 1898, letter from Samantha to Rosa:

Dear Children your letter came to hand last week and found us well… Uncle Sydney has been very sick for a week…Doc told them if he didn't take cold again and he had good care taken of him he thought he would pull through. [Doc] said it was the next thing to lung fever [pneumonia]. He has a very bad cough…Ad and Garnet have been in Columbus for three weeks. She was coming last week but Garnet took sick and she couldn't bring him home. I sell over a dollar's worth of butter every week. Cranston's give twelve cents for butter. Fisher gives fourteen cents and eighteen cents a dozen for eggs. I am afraid I won't get many eggs if it stays cold. Will is hauling fodder. He was scared about our pigs. Afraid they were taking cholera. He got some cholera medicine and put it in their slop. They seem to be well enough now. I don't know I will get to send this. I hope you will come down for Christmas. If Ike can't come to stay and visit, Rosa you can come on the train and he can come after you and help eat the gander. Ellis Figler went south with a man from Middleburg that is talking of trading for their land. Chickens are five cents a pound. Flicker says he is making money. [He] bought a new suit of clothes and a carriage. Mary's last chickens she sold brought her $10.00. I will close hoping to hear from you soon.

From your mother
S R McAdams

In the April 16, 1899, letter Samantha offers medical advice to Rosa.

Dear Children we received your welcome letter yesterday. Lester came from town. Mary and Lester made a garden and planted potatoes last week. I don't know when we will make a garden. The men want to get the sod plowed this week. I was sorry to hear Ike was sick after he went home. He had ought to take Hoods Sarsaparilla. Will says the horses can't stand the work this spring like they used to. I guess it is because he didn't work them much last winter. Lester and Mary went to Mrs. Sheneman's funeral Friday at Inskeep. She was staying there and was a sister of Wash Spain's. Loizze Adamson is dead. I guess Aerie [Clark] is poorly. I don't think she goes away from home. Parker is shaving getting ready for church. He bought a mandolin and is learning to play. We have lots of music. I cleaned out the pantry...my right arm and shoulder are lame...Graham didn't get to fix the wash house. Our white cow has a heifer calf...Will sold the 10 fat hogs last week. They brought over $55.00. The roan mare works good. They will get the sod plowed in a couple more days...The people are fishing in Darby [Creek]. Our cows are out on the road. I wish yours were with them and you were here to help me clean house. Parker says the young men are getting up a mandolin club. Edgar Holycross is going to get a guitar. Cloyd and George Burris have mandolins...the hand milks the cows in the evening but he doesn't get around very swift of morning…Hoping to hear from you soon I will quit writing as the men are coming in. We have Dutch cheese to eat once more.

From your mother
S R McAdams

Modern medicine of 1899 offered a variety of ointments and elixirs, including Hood's Sarsaparilla made by C. I. Hood Company in Lowell, Massachusetts. Samantha McAdams believed in the curing qualities. The following Hood's Sarsaparilla testimonial, advertisement, and ingredients are from cliffhoyt.com.

Do you suffer from torpid liver, scald head, pimples, rheumatism, gout, barber's itch, or That Tired Feeling? If you do, Hood's family of medicines would have had something for you. C. I. Hood & Co. turned out an amazing variety of medicines, but the standard bearer, and mainstay of the company for over half a century, was Hood's Sarsaparilla.

Mr. Hood reminisced about the beginnings of his company:

Forty-two years ago, after ten years of apprenticeship and ownership in an apothecary store, it occurred to me that there was a great opportunity for a business introducing a blood-purifying medicine with efficiency and economy as its base. With the ambition and exuberance of young manhood I earnestly determined to make this idea a livewire.

Fortunately, just at this time, a patient…brought to my drug store a prescription of unusual ingredients, which produced a remarkable cure for this customer, who had been a great sufferer from blood and nerve troubles…for several years…

I took this prescription as a base and perfected a formula for Hood's Sarsaparilla. The sale of this medicine surpassed all my expectations and made the name of Hood known in every city, town, and village in this country and also widely abroad.

Mr. Hood felt that the success of his medicine was due to his care in analysis and experiments conducted with "all the knowledge which modern research in medical science had developed." Taking the successful prescription, he added other well-known vegetable remedies. The ingredients of Hood's Sarsaparilla included the following:

- Sarsaparilla root—of great service for skin disorders, rheumatism, dropsy, and diseases of a scrofulous origin. (Scrofula is an enlargement of the lymph glands, with abscesses. It originates from tuberculosis. Many problems were due to a scrofulous condition of the blood.)
- Uvaursi—much needed by sufferers from kidney complaints, inflammation of the bladder, chronic diarrhea, diabetes, and troubles of a more delicate nature in either sex.
- Blue flag—especially recommended for scrofula, syphilis, glandular tumors, rheumatism, dyspepsia, constipation, and certain private diseases.
- Yellow dock—remarkable in its effect against scorbutic, cutaneous, scrofulous scirrhous, and syphilitic affections.
- Dandelion—a sign of hope for torpid liver, jaundice, depression, and melancholia.
- Gentian—useful for dyspepsia, loss of appetite, exhaustion, gout, and hysteria.
- Mandrake—without equal for constipation, scrofula, and skin diseases.
- Juniper berries—relieve suffering due to catarrh of the bladder, kidney complaint, and diseases of the urinary organs.
- Pipsissewa (wintergreen)—eminently useful for diseases of the blood, eczema, eruptions, rheumatism, gout, dropsy, and catarrh of the bladder.
- Stillingia—eradicates pimples, boils, abscesses, ulcers, syphilis, and chronic bronchitis.
- Alcohol (18 percent)—If the other ingredients didn't cure you, at least you wouldn't feel any pain.

The following is the May 6, 1899, letter from Mary to Rosa:

Dear Sister:

Received your welcome letter some time ago. Will now write a few lines in reply…Lester is planting corn. We have a pet lamb. It is blind in one eye. Trip [the dog] has a time after rats and rabbits…I have 92 little chicks and about 15 hens setting. I do not expect to set many more. I haven't set out any tomatoes or cabbage plants yet but expect to next week if the weather is fit.

Well, I took up the carpets and curtains and bed clothes and gave them all a good airing for about two weeks. Had the girl come over last Monday to commence to straighten up. We finished up yesterday noon. Today [stepdaughter] Hattie went to Marysville and hasn't come back yet so I had baking and everything to do. I'm about played out. This makes about four weeks of solid hard work for me. Last week the men came to mend the hedge fence. There were only four of them. They were here for four meals and overnight. I've had one or two hands to cook for ever since. So, you see it kept me busy with all the house cleaning and everything. I am tired and don't know hardly what I'm writing. Must close as it will soon be supper time.

Your sister, Mary

The following is the July 23, 1899, letter from Samantha to Rosa:

Dear Children your letter came to hand found me better. I feel better to-day than I have for over five weeks. I swept all the rooms and made the beds and got dinner. Hattie washed up all the dishes. The machine came at three o'clock yesterday. Commenced at four o'clock. Threshed 214 bushels of wheat. I think there will be 100 more to thresh in the morning. I don't expect them for dinner. Wheat is only 68 cents a bushel now. Lester stacked his wheat last week. Says he may not have it threshed for a month. We had 15 men for supper besides Will. I guess 3 went to Henry's [Clark]…Mary will can a bushel or two of blackberries this week. I thought I could do the work now but Mary says Hattie can stay another week. She is afraid I will get sick again. I am taking Dr. Pierce's Golden Medical Discovery…Brailey Sprague was buried last Sunday. Elmer and Etta are out on a visit. I guess we will send our buggy to town by Lester this week [and] have it painted and fixed…Serena Poling and Mr. Newlove in town are married…I ought to have 138 chicks. Put a spoonful of sulfur in your feed for lice. Some say the lice will leave in a week or so…The threshers are getting ready to thresh.

From your loving mother S R McAdams

Dr. Pierce's Golden Medical Discovery homeopathic remedy can be found in the Smithsonian Museum of American History. The uses for this product as provided on its packaging are as follows:

For the cure of all severe, chronic or lingering coughs, bronchitis, laryngitis, weak lungs, bleeding from lungs, public speaker's sore throat, hoarseness and suppression or loss of voice. A remedy for torpor of liver (generally termed "liver complaint" or "biliousness") and for habitual constipation of the bowels. For loss of appetite, indigestion and dyspepsia, and for general nervous disability or prostration, in either sex. An alternative, or blood purifier; valuable in all forms of scrofulous and other blood diseases. For skin diseases, eruptions, pimples, rashes and blotches, boils, ulcers, sores, and swellings, arising from impure blood.

Ingredients: Pure water, Borate of soda, Golden seal root, Queen's root, Stone root, Black cherry bark, Bloodroot, Mandrake root, Glycerin.

Avery Thresher used for harvesting wheat around 1899
(image from Wikimedia Commons)

Threshing separates the wheat seed from the husk. Once the wheat was threshed, the seed went to Lester Clark's cousin Andrew Beltz's grist mill to be made into flour. Though Samantha did not know it, her relative Ira Draper had the patent on the original mechanical threshing machine.

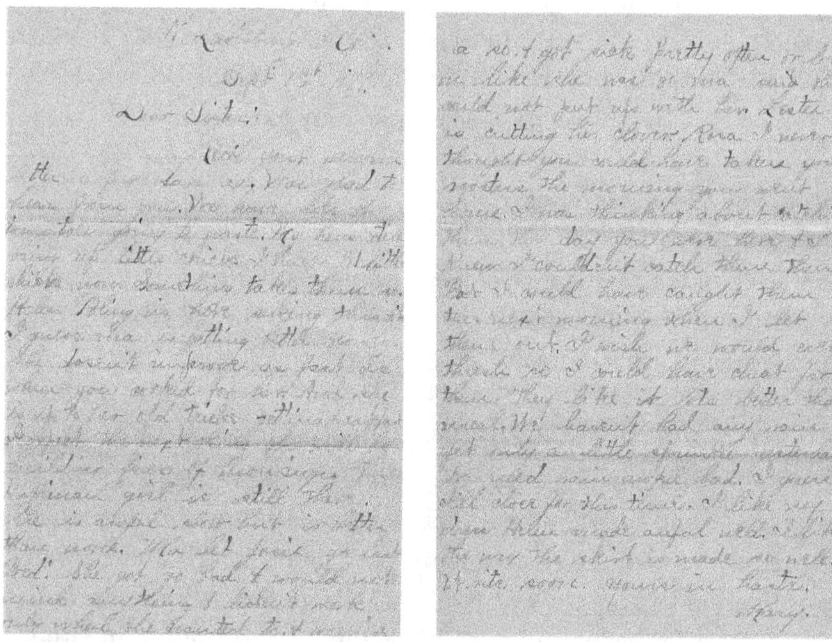

Mary wrote letters with a pen while Samantha and Rosa used a pencil. The September 1, 1899, letter from Mary to Rosa exhibits her thoughts written in her typical mistake-free style.

Dear Sister:

Received your welcome letter a few days ago. Was glad to hear from you. We have lots of tomatoes going to waste…Helen Poling is here sewing this week. I guess Ma is getting better slowly. She doesn't improve as fast as when you cooked for her. And she is up to her old tricks getting breakfast. I expect the next thing she will be building fires of mornings.

The Huffman girl is still there. She is awful slow but is better than none. Ma let Josie go last Wednesday. She got so bad and would not mind anything and didn't work only when she wanted to…She got sick pretty often or let on like she was, so Ma said she could not put up with her…

I wish we would ever thresh so I could have cheat for [my chickens]. They like it lots better than meal…We need rain awful bad. I guess I'll close for this time. I like my dress Helen made awful well. I like the way the skirt is made so well. Write soon.

Yours in haste,
Mary

Samantha wrote as she thought, as shown in her December 2, 1899, letter to Rosa.

Dear Children your letter came to hand found us about as usual. When I rest a few days, I feel pretty well and when I go to hard work, I get tired and feel like going to bed…We are going to have chicken for supper. I wish you could be here to help eat it. Mary has not been here for a week. She washed and ironed a week ago today. Will is chopping a lot of tops into firewood that Henry gave him. Lester stopped this evening. He got a letter stating Bell's had sold 80 acres of land for 10 dollars per acre. They sent him word they would go to Mansfield any day and have the man sign the deed. He wants over $40 now for sowing the wheat… Sade paid Henry Beltz 60 cents per bushel for apples. I expect you folks down for Christmas…Our cows are failing so on their milk. I only sold 5 pounds of butter this week. I sold over 8 pounds last week and got

15 cents a pound. I can't think of much more to write only be sure and come down.

From your mother
S R McAdams
Maybe you can come a day or two before Christmas and will [have] plenty for you to do.

The following is the March 3, 1900, letter from Samantha to Rosa:

Dear Children your letter reached us last week and found us about as usual…Our spotted sow had 7 pigs the 26th of last month. The black sow had 3. One dead and the others died. It was too cold for them…the hardware men brought a washer for us to try. The Queen. It turns with a crank like our churn. It is large size and can wash two quilts at one time in it. The price was $10 but it is the last one of that kind. They said we could have it for 6 dollars. Will washed the clothes in it Wednesday night. It was about half an hour from the time he commenced until they were washed and white clothes boiled and taken out of the boiler. This pretty day reminds me the time will soon be around when I have a work hand to cook for. We haven't taken the carpet up in the sitting room yet. Mary tacked carpet in the hall and fixed the curtains around the door. Henry has been staying home taking care of the baby [Jenny Clark, born July 24, 1899] as Miss Fisher didn't come back to work for them. Garnet and Sadie's children have whooping cough. There was an exhibition at Potter last night. Pearl Robinson has been going with Lulie Spain…Omer Inskeep was to see Hattie Sunday night. We hear Orlando is going to have a sale, quit farming, and going south to buy timber. Clifford bought the Brailey Sprague heirs land…Sadie stopped last night said she wanted to buy a cup of apple butter for her mother Eaton's sale. I will quit writing for this time. Write soon or come out before long.

From your mother
S R McAdams

The Queen washing machine, 1900

(image from Esty.com)

Late Victorian era hat styles

(*The Delineator* magazine, May 1900 issue)

The following is the April 29, 1900, letter from Mary to Rosa:

Dear Sister:

Received your letter a week ago and were glad to hear from you. Well I've been cleaning house all week. I have the sitting room, dining room and kitchen to clean yet. I expect to finish this week if the weather is good and nothing happens. I got lenolium. I don't know how to spell it but you know what I mean. Well I got it for the kitchen anyway.

I have 13 hens setting. The other hens bother my setting hens so. They break the eggs and mash the chickens. I am not having very good luck. I went to Marysville a week ago last Friday. I got me a white shirt-waist and a hat. They are not using feathers of any kind this summer. Everything is flowers.

Has Ike planted yet? Lester hasn't. The flies are making their appearance. I forgot to tell you we are cleaning house ourselves. I suppose you had all your work for nothing if you hadn't any company.

Lester went to Lima to the convention last Wednesday. Trip treed a groundhog under the crib and Lester helped him. Trip killed it. It bit him in several places. Trip was so stiff he could hardly go for a few days. The groundhog was as heavy as Trip. It was all he could do to carry it a few steps. We think he is a wonderful dog now.

School was out last Tuesday. Hattie didn't go the last week. She didn't want to take the examination.

I suppose Ma told you that Bell Holycross, Charley's wife, died suddenly. Hoping to hear from you soon.

I remain as ever, your loving sister,
Mary

The following is the May 29, 1900, letter from Mary to Rosa:

Dear Sister:

Will try and scribble a few lines in reply to your letter received a few days ago. We had a nice shower of rain last Sunday and it helped lots. Lester is plowing corn. His corn is very nice...

We went to the memorial service at U.B. Saturday night and to Potter[sburg] Sunday forenoon. We signed for a book about the life of D. L. Moody. I'm anxious to get it. We went to commencement at Lewisburg last Wednesday evening. Jennie Poling and five other girls graduated...

Our kitten killed a chicken. I got it away from her but it died afterwards. She doesn't offer to kill any more. I don't know whether we will have to carry her off or not. Lester says he believes his wheat is all cheat. Write soon.

Your sister,
Mary

Dwight Lyman Moody was an American evangelist and publisher connected with the Holiness Movement and the doctrine of a second work of grace leading to Christian perfection. His most famous quote was "Faith makes all things possible...love makes all things easy." He toured the country, drawing large crowds with a dynamic speaking style that preached God's love, friendship, kindness, and forgiveness rather than hellfire and condemnation.

The following is the June 21, 1900, letter from Samantha to Rosa:

Dear Children I will write you a few lines to let you know we are getting along...I was nearly sick for several days after you left but got to feeling so much better a week ago Tuesday...We went to Mary's to help butcher. I did not do much but I took cold. I am beginning to feel better. My shoulders and back hurt me. Lester got an electric belt to wear. He thinks it helps him. I have one but it made my back sore and I have only tried it twice. Mary had 55 pounds of sausage. We had 43 pounds. She fried 3 or 4 gallons and run lard over it. I put about 9 gallons in lard…Henry shipped his cattle to Cleveland a week ago yesterday. They wrote back. They got there in bad shape. One of the good cows was dead. Allowed him six dollars for her and our Jersey was crippled, got $23.00 for her. I think they paid $4.45 per hundred [pounds] for the best and $3.75 for the others. You ought to see how nice our new wind pump is…Ell Beltz told Will he had written his sister Retta and wants to move out here in house with his mother and Philip and we could farm together and he would not rent that corn ground. I guess Will rented a field of Lester's. They went to Marysville Friday and bought a new machine…I feel better than common today. I suppose it is because it is such a fine day…no more at present.

write soon to your mother
S R McAdams

The following is the September 24, 1900, letter from Samantha to Rosa:

Dear Children I will answer your welcome letter this afternoon…I have been so much better since it has turned cool. I have been taking Pink Pills. Am working all the time. I get up at 4 o'clock and am busy nearly all day…Albert came today to help haul manure. He will work a half a month and wants to husk corn. Such a time as the men have to get their corn cut. Lester has not got his all cut. Three hands came here the first of the week to cut. Said they would help through with it and backed out. Three more said they would come but didn't. Smiths finished the field here Friday and got done at our field at Lester's today…We have 105 hogs sold and the fat ones brought $68 dollars at 5 cents per pound… I went to town with Mary…I got calico and shirting for Will…I got me a pair of glasses and gloves…Ada Ziglar and man have come back to Snuffin's. He is cutting corn for Lester…Will paid his hands about 80 dollars. Lester thinks he will take some corn and some of Mary's chickens to the fair. He says he is going for three days…I have a very bad cold for a change…write soon.

From your mother S R McAdams

Samantha's Pink Pills were Dr. Williams's Pink Pills for Pale People, which, according to the Kansas Historical Society, was a patent medicine containing ferrous sulfate and magnesium sulfate. It was claimed to cure chorea, locomotor ataxia, partial paralexia, seistica, neuralgia rheumatism, nervous headache, the aftereffects of influenza, palpitation of the heart, pale and sallow complexions, and all forms of weakness in males or females.

Samantha put her doctoring hat on again in the January 24, 1901, letter to Rosa.

Dear Children your welcome letter came to hand last week. We were glad to hear from you. Sorry Ike had a headache. I thought Garfield Tea helped him when you lived here. We are about as usual. Your Pa thought he was taking la grippe the week you went home. He went to Dr. Emmons. He gave Will some tablets. He didn't get down with it but he took cold and has had a cough he is taking medicine for. It is better today…Henry Clark has bought Philip out. So, he owns the Beltz farm…Allie Reynolds is very poorly…Jenny Clark has been sick but is better now. Harry and Effie Caryl are tickled over their girl. His sister has a boy babe…Sam Bergandine is going to make sugar in Effie's camp next spring…so I will bring my letter to a close write soon.

From your mother, S R McAdams

Garfield Tea consisted of senna leaves and couch grass. Endorsed by President Garfield, the tea claimed to offer relief from kidney, stomach, liver, and bowel ailments. Some also used the tea to remedy headaches. Samantha was quite a fan of holistic medicines.

In the January 27, 1901, letter from Rosa to Samantha and Mary, Rosa inserted her monetary contribution to the family business.

Dear Parents and Sister:

I will write you a few lines this evening to let you know that I got home alright. Ike had the sick headache Saturday night and Sunday while I was gone. He has been having a bad siege of it today. I have ironed and made mincemeat today. I made some mincemeat Monday. I have four gallons. I worked awhile then bathed Ike's head awhile. His head has about quit. He is reading Peter Cartwright…

I am Sunday school teacher for year. Our saw mill will leave this week. There will be more woods left than I thought…Well I must close. Hoping to hear from you soon.

I remain your loving daughter and sister, Rosa Campbell

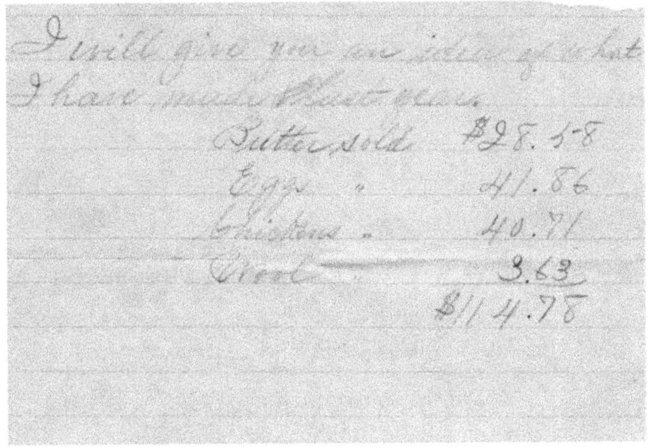

Rosa's income for 1900. Insert in her January 27, 1901, letter.

The following January 27, 1901, letter is from Rosa to Samantha and Mary:

Dear Parents and Sister:

We received your welcome letters yesterday. We were glad to hear from you. We are as well as usual. Ike has the headache a great deal. We went to Sunday school and church this morning. I teach the young women's class and have to be there at half past 9 o'clock. The Epworth League gives an entertainment tonight. I don't suppose we will go. It is snowing so hard…We are going to town today to have our pictures taken. It is a pretty day. I must close.

I remain your loving daughter and sister, Rosa Campbell

Lincoln Earl Clark, born February 12, 1901,

son of Lester and Mary Clark

The February 13, 1901, letter from Samantha to Rosa was full of the exciting news of the birth of Lincoln Earl Clark.

Uncle Ike and Aunt Rosa come out and see your new relative. Mary was taken sick Monday night. Lester stopped on his way to town for Dr. Emory. [He] wanted me to go home with him as he came back. The doctor thought she would not be sick very long and waited until twelve. She was so bad he went home for instruments. He said he didn't think the child could have been born alive if he hadn't used them. I never want to see another woman suffer as she did. He says the child is alright but I think sometimes it is doubtful. They are so tickled it is a boy. I stayed all night. I thought I was taking the grippe. Didn't sleep a half hour last night. The babe was so fretful. It seemed better this morning. Mary seemed to be getting along very well. They said to tell you folks to come down and see her fine boy. It weighed about seven pounds without its clothes. Your Pa has had another cold. I am so sleepy I can hardly keep my eyes open. Write soon.

S R McAdams

Earl's birth was announced in the *Union County Journal* on February 28:

Word comes from patriotic Allen that its leading Democratic politician, Lester Clark, organized a J.-J.-L. club of his own on the 12th inst, the anniversary of the birth of the immortal lover of liberty. On that day he enrolled one member, a black-headed, blue-eyed boy his excellent wife presented him. While his avoirdupois is not as large as the new steel trust, still seven pounds and lots of room to grow, is all right.

The following is the May 15, 1901, letter from Mary to Rosa:

Dear Sister:

Received your welcome letter last week. We are glad to hear from you. I expect you run yourself to death after your pet pigs. We have cleaned house but are not half done. I have 149 little chicks and three hens hatching. I've had awful luck with them hatching.

The baby weighed 15 ¾ pounds a week ago yesterday. I guess he is heavier now. He is the best baby. He only wakens once in the night and then goes to sleep in a little while. And here lately he lays on the bed half the time and plays. He notices things so much more so he can amuse himself…Daisy is still with me. She talks like she will stay all summer. I hope she will.

Earl's hair is still coming out. The new hair is starting to come in. He is so cute. He will hallow and laugh so much. I am anxious for the sleeper so I can take him outdoors…

We have had some hard freezes for this time of year. I suppose Ma told you Mattie Burroughs was working for her. Allie Reynolds is dead. I don't know any more to write so will close. Come out or write soon.

Your sister, Mary

The following is the July 28, 1901, letter from Samantha to Rosa:

Dear Children we received your welcome letter. We were glad to hear from you and hope you have got through with your hard work by this time. I expect you are about worked down. We are about played out. Will has been helping people thresh. I expect we will get our oats threshed next Tuesday afternoon. I have been doing the work for a week. Mattie has been sick. She was to have come last Sunday night. Will is going over this afternoon to see if she can come. If she can't maybe he can get Alice…Mary is not feeling so well. Forrest Jordans lost their babe last week…Mary wants you to see the baby in a long dress. They had his picture taken…Isaac just bundle yourself into your Methodist coat and come down and rest a few days. The darkies have a camp meeting… Write soon, come when you can.

Your mother
S R McAdams

The following is the October 20, 1901, letter from Samantha to Rosa:

Dear Children:

I will write to let you know we arrived home safe and sound…It rained a little sprinkle until we were almost to Newton. It rained a little harder after that. By the time we were on Johnson's Hill it was raining so hard we stopped in the [covered] bridge a few minutes. We did not get wet through. My navy blue coat is not soiled and it didn't make us sick…I hope Ike got over his headache. After we left, the horse cared at nearly everything along the road. My one legged chicken and cats seemed glad to see me. Levi Snuffin sold his hogs last week. Got $5.70 per hundred [pounds]. They are $5.75 now. Helen is done sewing for Mary. Alice Huffman is working there. Charlie has gone away again without marrying Mattie. He told her he owed for board and stay…I guess he was to come back in three weeks. Henry said the doctor thought Arie [Clark] would be able to come home before long. Clyde has been to see Hattie… Maybe she and Clyde want to get married. Rosa you ought to get cubebs and smoke in a clay pipe for your head. You must come out when you sell your hogs.

From your mother
S R McAdams

Cubeb pepper was smoked and inhaled to cure catarrh, hay fever, asthma, headaches, and head colds. Fifty-four-year-old Samantha was starting to feel the physical wear and tear on her body. She was quite astute in modern holistic medicine.

The following is the October 25, 1901, letter from Mary to Rosa:

Dear Sister:

Will write a few lines in a hurry. I suppose Ma told you Daisy was gone. Alice Huffman is here now. She does splendidly so far. We have been cleaning house. Helen Poling was here last week. Earl is feeling better. His gums have been hurting. He's the same old boy now…

I'm afraid to venture out to your place on the train as the scarlet fever and whooping cough is bad. Maybe we can drive out some day. That would be better than not at all. You folks come out.

Lester made a pen to put the stove in to keep Earl away from it. Earl gets right up in his high chair and stands alone or crawls out onto the table. He fell out of his buggy. He gets right up in it. I don't dare leave him any place only on the floor…

Effie and Harry were here a week ago Sunday for dinner. There was a man killed near here on the railroad. Come out or write soon.

Your sister, Mary

The following is the November 11, 1901, letter from Samantha to Rosa:

Dear Children your welcome letter came to hand last week. We were glad to hear from you. We have all had bad colds, something like la grippe, are feeling better this morning. Will is having a time keeping his men husking corn. If it don't storm, he thinks they will get done by Wednesday husking his share. Henry could not get hands to husk his corn. He wanted to sell his share in the field across the road. Will bought it. Is to pay fifty cents per shock and Henry gets the fodder. Lester, Mary, and Earl have had bad colds…He is getting another tooth. Earl was about sick with cold and his gums were swelled so. Maybe it would be best for Mary to keep him home while scarlet fever and whooping cough are raging. Sadie stayed all night here last Wednesday night. Garnet has been sick, has to quit school. Henry said Arie is home. They say she seems well as usual. Van Gordon moved in Henry's house last week. I have not got my kitchen cleaned yet. My back has been so lame since Thursday. I have not got much done. My arms have hurt so I was afraid to rise them very much…We were glad to hear you would get some more land. Will said it would be alright for Isaac to buy the farm since it joins your land. Will sold 15 fat hogs and sow…they brought $219.57. The calf brought 13 dollars. The corn in the field across the road averaged over a bushel a shock. The corn in the over field gives 2 bushel or more a shock. Will has a new wagon…I have given you all the news so will quit and get dinner.

Your mother
S R McAdams

Corn shocks are twenty to sixty stalks of corn bound by twine. The shocks are left standing in the field to allow the ears of corn to dry before being sold or stored.

The following is the November 11, 1901, letter from Samantha to Rosa:

Dear Children I will answer your welcome letter. We were glad to hear from you. We are about as usual. I have had a pain in my left shoulder. It is better today…I expect Isaac gets up before daylight to go on his new farm to work. Smiths went back on Will. He husked the last load of corn himself. He couldn't get anyone to husk and Henry took the corn back he bought of him. Will bought several loads of Rob Holycross and three loads of Milt Vance. Paid 53 and 55 cents per bushel. He has 100 shock of Philip Spain. He husks the corn, give 48 cents per bushel…If it's nice weather a day or two before Christmas you had better come then for it may be so cold you won't come…Hoping to see you soon.

From your mother
S R McAdams

Samantha received a reminder of her father's colorful life two years after his death. The *Marysville Tribune* had a "Do You Remember" column. The December 18, 1901, edition included the following:

Do you remember when Gid Draper walked out of the front door of the second story of the old courthouse, thinking he was on the ground floor?

The following is the January 25, 1902, letter from Samantha to Rosa:

Dear Children your welcome letter found us about as usual. Will is hauling fodder…I don't sell much butter. We got 24 cents a dozen for eggs last Saturday. Forest Bales had a sale. He is going to move to Bellefontaine to work on a train. McClung's house burned down a couple of weeks ago. Merle and Mr. and Mrs. Spain were here last Sunday night. Watson bought Old Jack. Gives 35 dollars for him. Will has hired the oldest Hammond boy to work in the spring. Chet Omer and Laura are married. Mary took Earl to church last Saturday night. Said he sat up and looked around. Seemed to enjoy it…I have got my calico dress made and two aprons. Have pieced another comfort top. Hattie is at Effie's yet. So no more at present write soon.

Your mother
S R McAdams

In her July 7, 1902, letter to Rosa, Mary wrote of the tragic Fourth of July incident in North Lewisburg.

Dear Sister:

While Earl is asleep, I'll write a few lines. I've been almost sick but I feel better now. I've often heard the second summer was the hardest on a baby but didn't realize what it was until now. Earl is cutting teeth and his bowels are loose. He was real sick for about two weeks. He was so bad he passed blood at times. We got medicine of Garwood and it didn't seem to help him. So, we got medicine of Wagstaff and he would not take that. So, then we went to Boylan and his medicine helped him from the first. That was in the cool weather and now it is so hot and he isn't well today. I'm worried about him. I got him a pair of red slippers and stockings and he is very proud of them…

Hannah Snuffin's mother is dead. Funeral yesterday…I expect you almost roast, cooking for hands in this hot weather. Willie Burroughs wife is dangerously sick. Has enlargement of the heart caused by riding her wheel so much.

There was a sad accident the 4th at Lewisburg. Sam Neal was drunk and sitting in front of Connell's grocery and wasn't harming anyone. Frank Connell gave John Marrow, 13 years old, a nickel to get a cannon firecracker and put it under Sam's leg. The boy did and they say they took a piece of firecracker out of Sam's leg two inches long. I heard he will lose his leg. Last night I heard blood poison had set in and he will die. Of course it was done in fun but they ought to have known better. They say Frank Connell was drunk. I don't know how true that was. I didn't know he drank.

People are mad at Frank about it and are talking about handling him. I guess he is paying Sam's expenses now. They say Mr. Marrow, the boy's father, whipped the boy terribly and went into the store to whip Frank and got behind the counter.

Guy Marks is home now. I saw him Saturday evening and didn't know him at first. Cliff Edwards died last night. Hoping to see or hear from you soon.

Your sister, Mary

The following is the August 7, 1902, letter from Samantha to Rosa:

Dear Children I will answer your welcome letter this afternoon as I am lonely. I have been waiting for you to come down but you have not come yet…I think I took cold being out in the air more than usual. I have been in bed about half the time this week, I am feeling a good deal better today as it is cool…We had 648 bushels of wheat. Our share was 380 bushels. I sold $14.90 worth of eggs last week. Our hogs don't have thrump anymore. Earl was very sick Monday night. The took him to [Dr.] Boylan. He is better…He looked bad but he is lively. It is his teeth and he is bilious. I heard Sadie went on the excursion to Niagara Falls. I expect I will be without a girl after this week. Chet Eatons have a young son. Come down instead of writing. I will take care of Ike's hat so he won't lose it.

From your mother
S R McAdams

The following is the August 7, 1902, letter from Samantha to Rosa:

Dear Children your welcome letter came to hand last Friday. Mary brought it and she left Earl here while she went uptown. Will went after the apples and cabbage Saturday morning. They are very nice… Will has been husking corn for hogs and put some in the crib. Lawrence Burris husked last week. He said he would come this week if they didn't move to Marion. I guess Hattie is home on a visit. Ebel Parker and Ina Burris went to Kentucky and got married. Phoebe told her she couldn't have any of her clothes. So she didn't go home, bought calico and made her dress. They are keeping house for a Mr. Sharp who lost his wife near Middleburg. Albert Parker has moved on Joseph Snuffin's place. Our corn is not very good. Will has spoke to Congrove for 100 bushels. The rain spoiled the fodder so it is not good. Some of the corn is so poor he thinks he will feed it to the heifers and cows…I expect you will be fixed up fine with your new barn and hen house…Ike Palmer is dead and old man Cooksy has been dry for two weeks. Elsie Asher has another girl babe. I didn't feel like going to the fair until Thursday. I wish I had gone. You said smallpox would be all over the country. I have not heard of any new cases. I will send you a dollar to get a bottle of medicine. Electric bitters tastes like your medicine. It is not so bitter. A large bottle is only 50 cents. Well I guess I have given you the news for this time.

From your mother
S R McAdams

Samantha kept up with her holistic medicines. Uses for Electric Bitters as provided on its packaging included the following:

The Great Family Remedy for all diseases of the stomach, liver and kidneys, biliousness, general debility, fever and ague, jaundice, blood disorders, and diseases of the urinary organs, neuralgia, nervousness and mental depression. As an appetizer they are unequalled.

Dose for an adult: Take from one to three tablespoonsful, three times a day, before or after meals, according to age and constitution of the patient. Weak and delicate constitutions should commence with one tablespoonful, reduced with sweetened water, and increase as the case demands.

The only listed ingredient is alcohol 18 percent (Smithsonian American History Museum).

Mary boasted about her abundance of winter supplies in her September 23, 1902, letter to Rosa.

Dear Sister:

Received both your letters and will write a few lines in reply. How about smallpox now? I don't know whether we will come to the fair or not. I would like to. Henry Clark is sick. I guess he has typhoid fever. The hat you brought for my collar, Helen says are called protectors. The diphtheria is bad around Lewisburg…

The cholera is commencing among my chickens again. I dug our sweet potatoes yesterday. They were very good. They were small. We bought 3 bushels of fine peaches for $2.10 a bushel…I canned 42 quarts and made preserves. I canned 76 quarts pears and then sold two bushel and still have some left. I have 205 cans of fruit. About 12 or 13 gallons jelly and jam preserves and about two gallons pickles. I want to make apple butter. Don't know whether I'll get to or not. I suppose it is of no use to ask you to come to the fair. Will close. Write soon.

Your sister, Mary

The following is the November 13, 1902, letter from Samantha to Rosa:

Dear Children we received your welcome letter. Were glad to hear from you. I have been in bed most of the time since Monday morning until to-day. We had to churn twice a week and I have been on my feet too much. Am feeling better today. Will has sold the black cow and jersey. Got $67.50 for them. Sold 21 hogs last week $5.65 [per hundred pounds]. They brought $231.65. Some were small. We were at Lester's Sunday afternoon.

Earl is lively as a cricket. We gave him a white hen and 8 chickens. She stole her nest out to the barn. Will has been husking corn. So much of the corn is spoiled. He thinks he will husk the balance of it. Only has 40 to 50 shock to husk. The diphtheria is raging near town. Some say it is membrane croup. Si Overfield's little girl died last week…I think you people will get rich before you know it, selling so much stuff. Isaac, put your new teeth in your mouth and new suit on and come down and visit your poor relatives. Lester leaves his teeth out of his mouth when he eats. I can't think of anymore to write so will quit for this time.

From your mother
S R McAdams
Write soon

The following is the November 20, 1902, letter from Mary to Rosa:

Dear Sister:

Will write a few lines in haste. I've been so busy I haven't had time to write. I just finished making Earl two dresses this afternoon. We are well and hope you are the same…Well we have had two rabbits 13 quails and 4 pigeons since the quail law has been in.

I suppose you have heard the <u>wonderful</u> news. They have struck <u>oil</u> at Lewisburg but [I don't know] whether it will amount to anything or not. The croup or diphtheria is so bad at Lewisburg I'm afraid to take Earl near there. There were 17 cases at one time and have been several deaths. Vallie Overfield's, nee Reams, little girl died with it. I think the Hedges have bad luck with their boys. Ma isn't very well. Henry Clark was able to go to town and took a back set and is in bed again.

Lester is husking corn. We haven't killed a pig yet. Earl is a regular monkey and does everything he sees anyone else do. He talks everything now. Christmas will be here soon. I suppose you folks will be out. I hear Earl rocking and singing. Must close and get supper.

Your sister, Mary

The following is the January 16, 1903, letter from Mary to Rosa:

Dear Sister:

Received your welcome letter a few days ago. Sorry you had to go home through the rain. Lester went to Mrs. Waddel's funeral that forenoon was the reason I didn't get down. I guess you will have to come out again this spring…

No wonder that water tasted bad. There was a dead rabbit in it. We have the other pump fixed now…We butchered last Wednesday afternoon. We killed 2 hogs and made 45 ¾ pounds sausage and 15 gallons lard. I had more casings cleaned than I needed…

Spring will soon be here. I must be looking for a girl. We had 4 little lambs but the colt killed one so that left us three. We had two in the house and Earl had a fine time with them. I dressed his doll yesterday and he was tickled as if it was new. Roy Grubbs and Bertha Congrove are married. Hoping to hear from you soon.

Your sister, Mary

The following is the February 14, 1903, letter from Mary to Rosa:

Dear Sister:

Received your welcome letter some time ago. Earl has been real sick and I have been so busy I haven't had time to write. He has had something like the grippe…I suppose you know Nate Howard is dead. Ella Epps isn't expected to live.

We killed a hen and made pot pie. Earl's birthday. He enjoyed it. We killed his two blue rabbits today and sent them down home for Ma to cook tomorrow and if Earl is well enough and weather fit, we are going to help eat them. We caught a Belgian hare the other day. If no owner comes for it, we will keep it.

Eggs are 15 cents [a dozen] this week. It is the most I got any day… Lester chops wood such weather as this as he can't husk corn.

I suppose you saw in the Journal last fall about Lou Spain's wife having him arrested and sent to the Pen. Well she got a divorce this winter and had a sale the day before he come back to pay the debts he made and she was security for. And then to cap all, she married him two days after he got back. What do you think of that? Write soon.

Your sister, Mary

Henry Clark, the McAdamses' landlord, had not been feeling well for quite some time. Looking to tidy up life's obligations, Henry made an offer to Will to purchase the farm. He also made Will a different offer to rent some adjacent property to farm. Will was concerned about costs and explored other options, much to Samantha's consternation. She was so upset that the wedding of Lester's daughter barely gets attention in the following letter to Rosa, dated April 30, 1903.

Dear Children I will write a few lines in answer to your welcome letter. I expect the carpenters have been at work on your barn and you have a lot of work to do. We are about as usual. The men commenced plowing in the field. Will is over to the place to help Sam haul manure. He rented 16 acres to Sam for corn across from Frank's old place. Henry is not getting along so well as he expected to. Willie Burris got sick. He has appendicitis. The doctor wants him to have an operation performed. He has part of his goods upstairs and took the balance of them to Allen Burris. He is going to town to the sanitorium as soon as he gets stronger. Congroves live in the house Willie lived in. Henry came here a week ago Sunday. Told Will he hadn't heard from Rye and would rent him the Milligan farm for 4 dollars per acre. 106 ½ acres and us to move this spring and only let us have it one year. I told your Pa I didn't like to pack to move well enough and no pay in it either. So, he said the next day we could stay here this year and he would put a hand in the other house if we rented it. Will told him he had so much work to do he wouldn't rent it. Moses Burris paid $3.00 per acre per year and was always in debt. Lester says your Pa would have made money on it. The money would have gone in someone else's pocket. Henry told Will yesterday he could have the 10 acres across the creek next to Herd's for corn. He has nearly $400 of our money and he thought if your Pa rented that farm, he had money in advance…Don't suppose your Pa will ever want to go anyplace besides Potter. There is so much work to do. He lays it on me and Mary. He's buying the place. It was the only land according to his talk that he could pay for. I wasn't thinking of the Elbert's farm and he went over there to buy it. I wanted him to buy Rob Holycross's farm. He said he would never get out of debt. A person has to have some place to live. He could have looked for a place last fall. Well as not I want him to fix the place up some and sell. He says he won't sell if he fixes it to suit him. Aaron Holycross's wife died last week. She had lung fever. She left five children. She was Frank Smith's girl. Sam says Graham's farm was sold for taxes. The youngest boy bought it. I suppose you read in the paper about Miss Clark and Carmean's wedding…I will bring my letter to a close. Hoping to see or hear from you soon.

From your mother
S R McAdams

Hattie Clark married Don Delboa Carmean on April 15, 1903. He was a partner with R. E. Kerr, selling goods in two Marysville department stores.

Marysville's *The Evening Tribune* advertisement, December 1904

The following is the June 11, 1904, letter from Mary to Rosa:

Dear Sister:

After so long I'll write a few lines in haste this evening. I haven't any girl and am taking music lessons so you see I'm busy from morning to night…We finished cleaning house a long while ago and the house is dirty again. We have had early garden truck for a long while. Our garden is all made now and looks nice. I had ought to have 400 young chicks but something takes them so bad. I don't suppose I have over 350. I have six hens setting. I'll not set anymore as I'll sure be out of coops.

We went to a children's meeting at Potter last Sunday. There is a children's meeting at the U. B. Darby tomorrow. Earl goes over to his grandpa's every week to stay all night. I think Earl is getting more teeth. He is so cross. I'll let Earl write a little. Write soon.

Your sister, Mary

Mary had done some homeschooling. Earl, age three years, four months, wrote to his aunt, "Aunt Rosa, Earl is a good boy. Kiss for Rosa & Uncle Ike. From Earl."

The following is the July 7, 1904, letter from Mary to Rosa:

Dear Sister:

After so long I'll answer your welcome letters received some time ago. We are having so much rain. Sarah Wilber's funeral is this afternoon. I canned 49 quarts of cherries. We didn't sell any. I had to quit taking music. I had to give it up. Earl has been sick and the work keeps me busy most the time so I had no time to practice. I took [lessons] of Ella Poling. She is a good teacher. Jane Bergandine hasn't been expected to live but is better now. She has dropsy…

I expect raspberries next Monday to tend to. The corn has come out wonderfully…My chickens keep dying all the time. I think it is indigestion. They were the same last summer…

Mother's girl is going to get married and leave her right when she needs her the worst. Earl is better but cross as a bear. Willie Burroughs have a big boy. Born last Sunday.

I suppose you saw in the paper about Don Franklin Carmean. Didn't that big puff about "The richest farmer of Darby Plains" kill you? Did you go anyplace for the 4th? We went to Lewisburg in the evening but there were no fireworks…Will close. I guess it's of no use to ask you to come out. Write soon.

Your sister, Mary

The following is the August 22, 1904, letter from Rosa to Samantha and Mary:

Dear Parents and Sister:

I will write you a few lines to let you know that I got home all right…I sold 22 young chickens and three hens the next day after I came home. Mr. Young didn't let me know that the buyer was coming until so late in the morning that I had let all my chickens out so I just sold what I could catch. I got 9 cents per pound for hens and 12 cents for chicks. They brought $9.91. The young chicks averaged over 38 2/3 cents apiece. Ike is talking of taking a load up to Marion in a day or so. My turkeys were all alive when I got home.

Isaac is hauling wood today. I done a big washing…I hope you didn't have threshers for supper. The train I came home on is due at Potter 11:36 standard time. That would be four minutes after 12 o'clock sun time…I must close, hoping to see or hear from you soon.

I remain your loving daughter and sister, Rosa Campbell

The following is the October 21, 1904, letter from Rosa to Samantha:

Dear Parents:

I expect you will be surprised to hear from me so soon but I thought I would write to you about John Cheney's place. He offers to take about $73 1/2 per acre. Of course, that is cheap enough the way land sells now but I know it would put you in debt even if you sold your place for $3000. There is 61 1/3 acres in his place. I wouldn't advise you what to do but thought I would write to you about it. Ike said if he could sell this place, he would buy it.

Ma, I was good and lonesome after you, Mary, and Earl went home. I expect you thought I was a great one not to send any for chicken supper. I don't know what I was thinking about.

I hope you got home safe. Write and let us know whether you think anything about buying the place or not.

I am going to the Aid Society this afternoon. Will make apple butter tomorrow.

Good bye from Rosa

The year of 1905 was eventful. Lester was raising his prize livestock, tending the crops, and helping Wilmer on his farm in Pottersburg. The *Marysville Journal-Tribune* printed an ominous article on May 23, 1905, to which there was no answer:

Mystery in Cattle's Death
Is Fatal Disease Prevalent in Allen Township or Have They Been Poisoned?

The mysterious death of four cows belonging to Lester Clark, of Allen Township, and one belonging to Mrs. Mary Burg, of the same neighborhood, has caused no little uneasiness to the farmers of that section. They fear that some terrible disease has come into their community to play havoc among their livestock.

The deaths among Mr. Clark's cattle occurred in rapid succession, and included his entire herd of milk cows. Several veterinaries have investigated the matter but are unable to diagnose the disease, if such it is, without a more thorough inquiry or post mortem.

The unusual circumstances of these deaths has caused fear among some of Mr. Clark's neighbors that his cows may have been poisoned, either by food of which they have eaten themselves, or which may have been administered by some unknown enemy in a spirit of revenge.

The matter should be thoroughly investigated. If it is a disease which has come along the cattle, measures should be at once taken to stamp it out; or if there is any good grounds for the poison theory the perpetrator should be discovered and punished to the fullest extent.

The following is the October 21, 1905, letter from Mary to Rosa:

Dear Sister:

After so long I'll write you a few lines and let you know we are well and hope you folks are the same. I finished cleaning house last week. Lucy Huffman helped me [for] four weeks. She is only 13 years old but big and stout and lots of help.

Earl is in the cornfield helping Pa load corn. I guess Pa has the most of his corn out. Lester has gone to a sale. He bought a sleigh at Shep Clark's sale. So, I suppose we will sleigh ride snow or no snow.

Earl and I were in Marysville Tuesday. I picked a wardrobe for mother. She told me to get her one. I got me a new coat. I like the styles for this winter. I got my glasses exchanged the next week after the fair but they didn't suit so I changed them Tuesday again…

I'm trying to learn my young chickens to go to the hen house. I dread to see winter come…I have 18 little leghorns hatched out. I expect I'll have to knit them some stockings. Will close. Write or come out soon.

Mary

Samantha and Wilmer McAdams moved a half mile south of Pottersburg, Ohio, in 1905 and rented a farm that Lester Clark had purchased. Their farm was a dairy farm with field corn to feed the cattle. Samantha was tired of transforming the new house into a home.

The following is the November 6, 1905, letter from Samantha to Rosa:

Dear Children after a long delay I will answer your welcome letter. I am tired out taking care of milk and doing everything myself. Ez Organ hauls our milk. Comes every other day and on Saturday. Commenced hauling ours last Wednesday. We got 9 crocks of milk every day. I sent nearly 10 pounds butter to Lewisburg Saturday. Got 18 cents at Fisher's. It is only 16 cents per pound at Potter. Will has got his corn all home and in the crib. Had about 650 bushel, his share. Gamble and George Smith are to commence digging a ditch in the back part of the place today and Will is going to haul dirt on the ditch in the orchard and haul gravel for the barn lot. He has a pipe laid from the tank to straw shed for the cattle to have water this winter. Lester's were here yesterday. Earl says he don't care what Old Santa brings but his engine is about played out and he would like a new one. Lester is afraid Herrick will be elected. We got a letter from Aunt Marion and said Midlam was going to vote for Pattison…My hens have about quit laying. I only have 3 dozen for Lane this week. I have sold a few old hens and let Mary have 15 pullets. I think I will sell a few young roosters. Your Pa says he is going to kill a hog before long. I have been making an outing flannel dress…Write soon and come whenever you can.

From mother
S R McAdams

Lester took a wagonload of Wilmer's crop to the train station to be transported, when his team of horses spooked. He was pinned under the wagon. His injuries included a broken shoulder, broken ribs, a sprained neck, and contusions. The *Marysville Journal-Tribune* wrote of the accident on

December 28, 1905. Don Carmean, mentioned in the article, was Lester's son-in-law. He was the owner of the large dry goods and department store in Marysville.

Lester Clark's Narrow Escape

Lester Clark, of Allen Township, who had a narrow escape from death last Saturday in an accident at Pottersburg, is reported to be recovering nicely. Mr. Clark was engaged in unloading corn from his wagon into a car on the Erie track, when his team started and he was thrown under the wheels, one of which ran against his neck. It took seven men to lift the wagon off his body. Only the stoppage of the team prevented his neck from being broken. As it was his shoulder was dislocated and his face was painfully bruised. Mr. Clark is the father of Mrs. Don Carmean, of Marysville.

The following is the March 12, 1906, letter from Samantha to Rosa, announcing good news:

Dear Children I will write again to tell you about the little girl babe at Lester's. It was born Friday eve. Alf Reams's wife died, Alice's aunt. The funeral was Saturday. Lester brought Earl over about 3 o'clock as Alice wanted to go away to the funeral the next day. When he got back Mary was in bed and he went after Mrs. Turpin. Telephoned for [Dr.] Boylan. She and babe seemed to be getting along well as could be expected. The babe weighed 9 ¾ pounds. It looks as plump and large as Earl did when he was a month old. Earl said he didn't know what to think of it. He said take it away. He didn't want it. But after a while he got on the bed and kissed it. Said he thought it was nice. Said he was so disappointed because Mama was in bed. He didn't know what to do…I hope you can come down. The babe looks more like Mary than Earl did…Lester seemed quite pleased over his girl. Write soon.

Your mother
S R McAdams

Florence Rose Clark, born March 9, 1906,

daughter of Lester and Mary Clark

Samantha pointed out Will's fatigue of his job in a May 23, 1906, letter to Rosa. He was getting tired and depressed.

Dear Children I will write to let you know we are about as usual. Lester planted our corn over here last Thursday. Earl was here. He had a time playing with Lily. He got a frog and played with it in a tub of water…we were over to Darby Sunday. You ought to have been there. The babe was in good humor and laughed and had a fine time. She looks around more now. She is fatter than ever. Her hair is getting thinner on the side of her head. She is a fine babe. Earl goes like the wind on his wheel. Mary put his new suit on him. He looks nice in it. Has a white collar and white hat. It is Russian style. Will thinks the oats will not be very good unless it rains soon. My hens lay good now. I make butter to sell. It was only 15 cents per pound at the store last week. I expect we will clean the sitting room tomorrow. We washed the blankets yesterday. Lucy ironed this morning. Clara Grey has a boy. Arnise is back and Laura and little girl came last week. Will's sister Nancy has been poorly again. Eggs were

14 cents a dozen last week. The Marysville peddler comes on this road. Will is oiling harness. He has been discouraged as usual. Said he would sell out. I suppose he will never rest until he gets rid of the farm and then he won't know where to go. I wish you folks were here for dinner. I am going to have beans and fat meat. Well good bye. Write soon.

From your mother
S R McAdams

The following is the July 24, 1906, letter from Samantha to Rosa:

Dear Children I will answer your welcome letter this afternoon. We are about as usual. I washed this morning. Was about played out after dinner but I went to bed and had a nap so I feel rested. Will has gone to heath after the calves he had in the pasture. We had a big rain and thunderstorm Sunday night. And it rained yesterday morning. We are having too much rain. They got the grass all up at Lester's. They were here Sunday, were well. I wish you could see the babe now. She is so plump and nice. Her hair was all curled on top of her head. It is coming in on the sides of her head. Her eyes are bright blue. I guess Lester will cut our oats tomorrow if it don't rain. Well I have not got my kitchen papered yet. Ken Spain says now he can't come unless your Pa goes after him. Will went to Marysville yesterday afternoon. He said he didn't see much difference in Nancy, only she seemed weaker. Her bowels got better the next day after we were there. I took cold coming home that night and have been so nervous and run down all the time. It is first one thing then another…I wish you folks could come down while our old place looks green…Mollie Underwood is visiting her folks yet in Hardin County. I have not been to Lib's since she went home with Eva. Sam's other cow had a calf. Sadie is going to teach the Potter school. Lucy will teach in the brick school house in Henry's district. I hope Ike is feeling better. Come down if you can.

Write soon to your mother
S R McAdams

Wilmer's sister, Nancy McAdams Overfield, died two weeks later. The following is the November 7, 1906, letter from Mary to Rosa:

Dear Sister:

After ever so long, I'll write a few lines. We are as usual and hope you are the same. I've been so busy. I didn't have time to write…I got mother's tablespoons. They were $3.50. If you want to, you can get Pa shoes and let my share go on to your share of the spoons. Mother is just worked down.

Nella [Mary and Lester's live-in housekeeper] and Earl are pulling turnips. Earl has a bad cold. He has pants on now. Lester is hauling corn. The corn is good this year. Pa is hauling from here. He has the most of his corn out.

The baby has only two teeth. She is such a baby to talk. She crawls by rolling. Whenever she wants any place, she rolls. She will be 8 months.

I suppose Brodrick is elected. Les Cline was elected Commissioner. We have a phonograph. We have 48 records. The most of them are good pieces. I guess we will never tire of it. We have had it about a month. Earl thinks there never was anything like it…

Put sweet potatoes away today. We bought 19 bushels of Irish potatoes of Glen Asher. They were fine ones. Wasn't that terrible about his boy? We have lots of apples in our cellar. We have killed 69 young chickens since the last of July. Can you beat that? I have shirts to make for Lester…

Earl seems to like school books. I've been learning him out of the first reader. Was that Mrs. Hoxworth's sister that was burned so she died? I saw in the paper it was Etta Grooms and I thought Mrs. Hoxworth's sister was that name. I must close as the man has come after Earl's old iron.

Write or come out soon. Your sister, Mary

Wilmer was tired from the physical demands and mental stress of farming. Even so, he finally bought his own farm. He and Samantha bought thirty-six acres from Howard Beltz on Marysville Road just east of town. The old mill creek flows through the front third of the property. Wilmer paid

$4,320 cash, the 2020 equivalent of $119,000, for the farm. Lester rented the Pottersburg farm to Mr. Heildreth and also had farms rented to sharecroppers in Logan County and Champaign County.

The following is the November 14, 1907, letter from Samantha to Rosa:

Dear Children I will write a few lines to let you know we arrived home safe and sound. The men were waiting for us. It was about one o'clock. When we got home, we had our valises checked but they did not come until evening. Will saw Nella out with Florence Tuesday. She said Earl was at school. Will hauled a load of corn yesterday afternoon…Today is the day the peddler comes. I only have 11 eggs. I expect you have your house clean by this time…Will is husking corn here this forenoon. He will go to Lester's after a load in the afternoon. I looked in your Pa's hat. It is size 6 7/8. I expect about 7 would do for the cap. I hope Ike didn't have a sick spell after we left…How do you like your range by this time? Write soon.

From your mother
S R McAdams

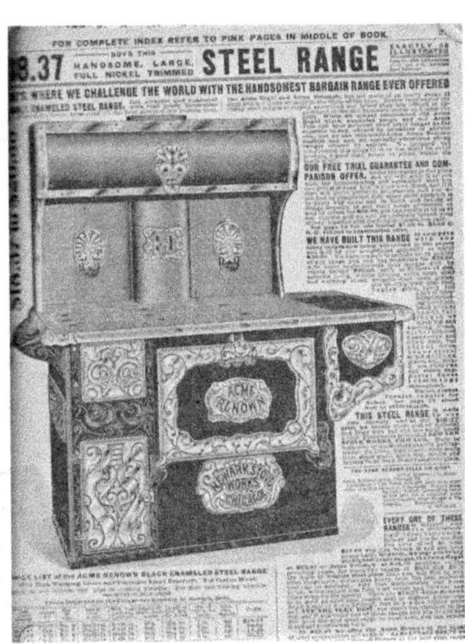

Coal-fueled cook range in a 1905 Sears catalog is similar to Mary's new range that Samantha mentioned in her letter.

The following is the February 2, 1908, letter from Mary to Rosa:

Dear Sister:

I will write a few lines as we are at home today. I am uneasy about Ma. I haven't heard from her since last Sunday and she was sick with the grippe. She looked so bad and coughed so. I guess she was like we were. Earl was sick. We had the doctor for him Thursday forenoon. He had a bad sore throat. I guess he is like I used to be to have a sore throat so often. The baby seems to feel good today. She has a cold.

Wasn't yesterday a scorcher? How is Ike getting along? Last night was the coldest night yet. Nella goes to Aerie's Tuesday. I expect Mae will come to East Liberty on the train Wednesday morning for us…Earl has been going to school regularly for two months or more but if it stays cold this month, I don't suppose he will go much. Nella can hardly wait until she gets to Henry's. I get so disgusted with Nella. The last week she seems to think she is already of age. The children are bothering me so I will close.

Hope you folks are all well. We are tolerable, well, except Earl. Write or come out when you can.

Your sister, Mary

A clipping Mary sent to Rosa

The following is the February 20, 1908, letter from Samantha to Rosa:

Dear Children I will write a few lines this afternoon to let you know how we are getting. I am about over my cough and feel a good deal better than I did when I wrote you before. Will is well as usual. He got Danna to help him saw an old apple tree this afternoon. The teacher stayed all night here a week ago Monday night. She didn't send word to Oba's she was coming and Tuesday eve they lit on to her. Said there was a plot to get her to leave. They said so much she got mad and left the next morning. I told her I was not able to board anyone. She has gone to Dannie's to board. They were here Sunday night. Ralph came to the door and asked if Nella was here. I have not seen her since she went to Henry's. Mary has not been here since I wrote you the last letter…I was very sorry to hear Ike had his bad spells again. Maybe he ate too much of something that was against his stomach. The children and Mary were here yesterday. The children are better. The doctor said they had catarrh fever…Nella came bouncing in yesterday afternoon. She wanted to exchange books with me. Said for me to give my book to Merle today as she was going to town…Aerie has her in the Methodist church. She ought to be alright. Clara Holycross's little girl has whooping cough. I expect Royal Beltz will make our porch as soon as it gets warm enough to work at it. Will is splitting wood. Athey's sale was last Tuesday. They are going to Michigan. Daisy never came back to wash for me. Howard Beltz bought a pool room up town…One of our cows is about dry and the other don't give much milk. I have 21 eggs in the basket, the most I have had since November. I have rheumatism in my arms. I thought I rest up today and wash tomorrow. I have a line stretched upstairs so I don't take quite so much cold of washday. I guess I will have to quit writing. So good bye. Write soon and come when you can.

From your mother
S R McAdams

The following is the March 4, 1908, letter from Mary to Rosa:

Dear Sister:

After so long I'll write a few lines. We have been sick so much. I haven't had time to write sooner. Earl was sick when I wrote you last and he got better. Then the baby was very sick with catarrhal fever then she was well. Earl took sick again and, in a few days, Florence was sick also. So, they were both sick at once to take care of. They are better now but not well yet. I am almost sick with a sore throat. I guess I got it from the children.

May came 4 weeks ago today. Nella left the night before May came. I guess Harry is having a time with her from what I hear. She runs with the lowest trash in Lewisburg. May is very neat about her work but she is slow...

Was sorry to hear of Isaac's sickness. I've been thinking of calling you over the phone but the baby is cross so much I was afraid I wouldn't get to talk if I did get you. Florence has the earache so much and is so cross and I've had my hands full.

I'm so glad to see nice weather. Our cellar has water in it. I sometimes think some of our sickness is caused from the cellar and water we drink from these wells. I'll not send Earl to school until it is more settled as he came home with his feet wet every night for ever so long. It was no wonder he was sick.

I get so discouraged with so much sickness. It will soon be busy season and I dread it. If we would stay well, I would be glad to get the dirt cleaned up, but when we are sick, I can't get anything done.

Have you set any hens yet? None of mine want to set. They have just commenced to lay good.

Lester has rented the place he got of Pa to a man by the name of Heildreth from the Beechwoods. I guess they have several children. Lester is trimming some of the trees today. Write or come out soon.

Your sister, Mary

The following is the March 23, 1908, letter from Samantha to Rosa:

Dear Children I will write to inform you of your father's safe return from your place. It must have been three o'clock when he got to Lewisburg. He is sowing grass seed…I suppose you have all your plans laid for the summer and hate to leave there as you have fixed up so. Maybe you can get a hand this spring. Do as you think best about coming down to stay here. The teacher went to Henry's Friday eve and stayed until this morning. Nella, the teacher, and Jennie Clark were here yesterday afternoon. Nella has got Mary's silk dress. Maybe she will be satisfied now. We have been to John Spain's and Dannie's. Mary heard Em Spain's mother was not expected to live. Mr. Heildreth has moved on our old place…I hope I will see you coming down soon. I was glad your Pa took notion to visit you even if he didn't stay long. The teacher and I got along all right. I will have to quit writing and get to work. My back has been hurting me a deal for the last week. Write soon.

From your mother
S R McAdams

The following is the April 3, 1908, letter from Samantha to Rosa:

Dear Children I will write you a few lines this afternoon. We have a light attack of la grippe. Will took a chill a week ago tonight on going to bed and was sick all the next day and Sunday night and Monday. I was sick, didn't even sweep the floor. I washed Wednesday, baked light bread yesterday, and ironed this morning. Mary went to town a week ago Wednesday, got a new jacket and black silk dress. May and the children stayed. They were not well. All of them had grippe again… Everybody that has to move must be on the move. So many wagons are on the road with goods this week. Today is the peddler's day. He paid 13 cents a dozen last week. My hens are doing better. We got 24 eggs last night. Royal has not got to work on the porch yet. His wife and mother were here one afternoon. She said she told him that she was not going to stay there much longer and he had spoke for George Spain's house up town. She seemed so pleased over it. School is out two weeks from next Wednesday. The teacher is coming here to stay until Saturday after her school is out. The board meets that week so she would get an order for her money…I was glad to hear Ike was better. I suppose he is thinking of the money he is going to make on his horses and that keeps him up better. Will Holycross and wife stopped one evening for us to go to Andy Beltz's…The teacher and Clara came over Tuesday morning to see if there was anything she could do. Lee Zieglar was playing ball Sunday and Eva Snuffin run up behind him as the bat went back. It knocked her down and broke several teeth. The doctor thought she would get well. So, write soon.

From your mother
S R McAdams

Home of Mary Clark in 1908, with Earl, Lester, Hattie, Florence, and Mary

Home of Samantha McAdams in 1908, with Rosa Campbell, Earl
Clark, Isaac Campbell, Samantha, and Wilmer McAdams

The following is the May 28, 1908, letter from Samantha to Rosa:

Dear Children we received your welcome letter. Sorry to hear of Ike
being sick. I hope he is feeling better. I am feeling ever so much
better as the men finished painting the house this forenoon. They
are going over the barn a second time. Your Pa is helping. He wants
to get it done tomorrow. The barn is canary color trimmed in Nile
green. The house is all white. You won't know the little place when
you come the next time. Clara washed the lower windows and
cleaned rooms down stairs. Mary was here yesterday. She cleaned
woodwork and swept upstairs. She got her house cleaned…Florence
is still learning to talk…Earl and May caught some small fish…He
went to Sunday school two Sundays. He is going to speak at the children's meeting the third Sunday in next month. My red roses are out
and my locust tree is in bloom. I will have a few peaches and cherries
and plums if they don't fall off…I had nearly 11 dozen eggs today.

Got 14 ½ cents a dozen. Well it is supper time and I must bring my letter to a finish…Will has a new riding plow. Mary is thinking of having Grant Beltz take the picture of their house one of these days. John Bergandine and Mrs. Dunbar are married…Write soon and come when you can.

From your mother
S R McAdams

The following is the June 21, 1908, letter from Samantha to Rosa:

Dear Children your letter came to hand last week. We were glad to hear from you. I hope Ike will not have his sick spells so often now. The chickens and birds got all the cherries on the small tree…Will wants to know how far along your rye was when Ike turned his hogs in the rye field and how many your Pa ought to turn on the 10 acres of his rye and how soon Ike thinks it would pay better maybe than feeding them corn. It is thin on the ground. I guess some of it froze out. Earl has been here 3 days. Your Pa took him home and I went along. Mary brought me home. Her rooms look different than they used to…Our garden is good and potatoes are fine, will soon have new ones if the chickens don't scratch them out. My hens have about quit laying again. The jersey cow had a calf. We are going to sell the milk. I have been lame in my right limb since I wrote you but am better again…Florence is talking right along. She is real cute but is getting tanned. She don't like to wear her bonnet. I ought to have 94 chicks. They run around so I can't count them. They are all healthy…I wish you could come down. Maybe we will have peaches and plums to can and you can come. So, write soon.

From your mother
S R McAdams

Earl, Florence, and Mary, 1908

The following is the November 12, 1908, letter from Mary to Rosa:

Dear Sister:

I will write a few lines in haste. I am completely discouraged about Ma's teeth. I am afraid if it depends on me to take her, she won't get them for whenever she can go I can't and when I can go, she can't. I wanted her to go a few weeks ago but she didn't want to go then. So last week I went for her and she was about sick and couldn't go. Then we intended to go yesterday and she sent me word not to come until today.

Last night Florence had the croup and I can't take her out today. So, I sent her word I couldn't come. This seems like winter. We all have bad colds. Earl is almost sick with a cold but he goes to school. He studies the Second Reader, Drawing, Writing, Arithmetic, and Spelling. I was at school one afternoon when they spoke pieces. Earl spoke the piece you gave him…

We bought the Chase piano. We intend to fix the house if the hands ever get to it. They promised a month ago. The trimmers are trimming the porch and bay window…We are going to put a slate roof on. The hands are to commence in the morning if the weather is fit…I got the hands to cook for.

I got me a new breast pin and beauty pins for shirt waist. Earl is doing fine in his studies this term. The teacher boards at home yet. She seems very nice. May goes to school. Florence is cutting paper. She cuts paper by the hour.

Two of the prettiest kittens come here. They are about half grown. They are spotted. White, black, and yellow. Earl has one and Florence has one. Florence thinks so much of hers…I must get dinner. Write or come out.

Your sister, Mary

The following is the November 12, 1908, letter from Mary to Rosa:

Dear Sister:

Will take a little time to write a few lines. How are you folks? The children and myself have bad colds. The teacher hasn't commenced boarding yet. She talked some of it this week. But it got nicer so she still goes home. Earl has not missed a day or been tardy yet. He is in a language class now. He found an old skate at Pa's last Sunday and has been skating on one skate…

Florence has had a toothache and the last week she had rheumatism. She complained so much Lester went to the doctor and got medicine for her to take and liniment to put on her legs. She kept me busy yesterday doctoring her. She seems better today.

I try to sew but we get up so late I can't get much done…I have two dresses for myself and two for May and four for Florence and two big aprons to make. Suppose I'll get through before warm weather.

I went to Dr. Creviston about my face. He said it was eczema. His medicine seemed to help it. I guess none of the rest got it. If they did, we could not tell it…

Earl just got home. He says he has 53 head marks now. The teacher missed putting a few down or he would have had more. Whenever we ask Florence where Aunt Rosa or Uncle Ike are, she says "on the train." We butchered the day you went home. It is getting late so will close and get supper. Write soon.

Your loving sister, Mary

The following is the January 21, 1909, letter from Samantha to Rosa:

Dear Children we received your welcome letter and were glad to hear from you. We were well enough to go to Columbus. Mr. Holycross has been sick since Tuesday. Will butchered the sow Tuesday. Henry Beltz, Andy and wife, two of her sisters from Indiana, the Dannas, the teacher, and Mrs. Holycross were here for dinner. We have a lot of lard. I put down two gallon of sausage. Mary and the children came over in the sleigh Sunday. Florence had been having the toothache. Earl had a cold. He had been out in the snow so much. The teacher had not been there yet. I sold over five dollars' worth of eggs since you were here. I only got 5 last night. It has been too cold weather for them for a week or so. I wish you folks were here to help us eat fresh meat. I ironed this morning and don't feel like working since I have got the grease cleaned up. Some of the folks have had a fine time sleigh riding. Your chickens seem to enjoy their new home. I don't think any of them lay. Aba Spains are out in their sleigh 3 or 4 times daily. I guess Surge Spains will not go west. His wife was here yesterday. She spoke for a gallon jar of lard. I guess I have given you all the news so will quit writing and get dinner. So good bye. Write soon.

From your mother
S R McAdams

Mary Clark and her travel buggy

Mary and Lester's house on Inskeep-Cratty Road needed a new roof and repairs. The family moved to the Pottersburg farm for two years while the work was being done. Lester was so busy with his work and politics that he didn't have much time for Earl and Florence. Earl, very close to Grandpa Will, spent the majority of summers with his grandparents.

Isaac's headaches got worse. He acted erratically and at times irrationally. Ike had made some poor decisions, and that concerned Rosa greatly. Rosa did not write for the next two years. Troubles in her life at times overwhelmed her.

The following is the January 7, 1911, letter from Mary to Samantha:

Dear Mother and Father and all:

I'll write a few lines to let you know we are well and hope you are the same. We butchered Tuesday and had a fine day. We got lard done and sausage ground before supper and stuffed the sausage after supper. I had lots more casings cleaned than we needed. We had 44 pounds sausage and 9 gallons of lard. The sausage, ribs and backbones are froze. So, I guess they will keep awhile.

Florence was riding on her sled today. My flowers got nipped. Lester was so afraid I would burn a piece of coal more than necessary. So, the dampers were shut. We surely have been having winter…

Our pigs are growing. Earl gave them plenty of straw and they knew how to fix it. He hates to start school tomorrow. School will be out before we know it. Earl keeps busy carrying wood since it is so cold. I keep fire in the kitchen all day. The little boy that got hurt in town died last Monday.

I guess I must close and do my chores. It keeps me busy heating water and thawing ice. Our pump to well has got so we can't use it. The men thought they would be here this week to fix it. I must close. Write soon.

Lovingly, Mary

The following is the February 18, 1912, letter from Mary to Samantha:

Dear Mother and Father and all:

We arrived home safe and sound. Maude [the horse] brought us home about a half an hour quicker than she took us up there. She got tired before we got home though. She was ready for her supper. I didn't have to get out to lead her through the bridge. She went herself by talking to her. Florence is in the Morris rocker asleep. Earl is sleepy but waiting for me to read *The Stockman* to him.

It is 8:30 o'clock and I got my work done. I had to cook supper and put things away. All but my coat. I guess all the hairs of the robe are on it…That O'Brian I told you was burned so bad is to be buried over here tomorrow.

Earl wants me to stop and read that story so he can go to bed. He wanted to ride Maude tonight. I guess I'll close. Hoping to hear you soon.

Lovingly, Mary

Florence, Earl, Trip the dog, and Maude, 1912

The following is the April 14, 1912, letter from Mary to Samantha:

Dear Mother and Father and all:

Received your letter a few days ago. Was glad to hear from you. I expect you are very clean up there. I haven't anything done and don't know where I'll get started to cleaning. Florence has had a time with her heel. She hasn't worn her shoe for a few days until this morning to Sunday school…Earl and Florence drove home from Sunday school alone. Maude tried to run off with me in town last Tuesday. She got scared at a wheelbarrow. I guess she has had too many oats and condition powder…

I have about 50 geese eggs. I am afraid they will spoil…I cooked the last of our beef today. We got our smoked meat home but it isn't smoked anything like we always smoked it. I'm afraid it won't keep long. But I expect we will soon use it up. The pigs keep getting out so we can't let them run out much. Earl fixes a place in the fence then they find another. They don't take near the corn and do so much better. I wish we could let them out all the time. I must close. Write soon or come down.

Lovingly, Mary

Left to Right: Isaac and Rosa Campbell, Mary Clark, Samantha and Wilmer McAdams, Florence Clark (in front), 1912

The following is the January 1, 1913, letter from Mary to Samantha:

Dear Mother:

I will write a few lines. I was sick Sunday night and all day Monday. I was in bed the most of the time. Lester and Florence did most of the work that was done. I guess I had the grippe. I was afraid Earl and you folks would have it. I think that is what Florence had as she complained of her head so much. I thought my head would almost kill me at times. I washed yesterday and I guess I took a little fresh cold. I wished I was at your house for you to wait on me…

Monday Florence stayed right with me. She cried most of the day. She said she was afraid I would die. I guess that was the first day I ever failed to be able to work since she can remember. We got home 2:30 Sunday. Everything was dirty and I had the blues Monday. I haven't cleaned very good yet…

We have to begin to think about the time Earl had to come home. The bells were ringing downtown at midnight last night and woke me up…Hope you are all well.

Lovingly, Mary

The following is the January 25, 1913, letter from Mary to Samantha:

Dear Mother and Father and all:

Will try to write few lines this evening in reply to your letter received a few days ago. We expected to come out to your place today but Florence is sick and I was afraid to risk taking her so far. She hasn't been very well for a week or so. But Thursday night, yesterday, last night and today she feels awful bad. I think it is the grippe. This is the worse she has been since we moved…

It's nice weather and we are well enough maybe we can come next Saturday. I expect you looked for us today. The day Pa brought Earl, Ezra Burroughs was here for dinner. He is holding meeting at Mt. Zion. I guess he is having pretty good meetings…

Lester bought a red rooster at the poultry house. So, we have two red and two Plymouth rock roosters. It got so muddy where the pigs were that we had to put them in the barn. They are growing and doing nicely…

Lester bought a white hog at the stock yard. It weighed 220 pounds. Was awful fat. We butchered it last Tuesday. We got about 8 gallons of lard and only 24 ½ pounds sausage. The sausage is awful fat. I guess that will end our butchering this year. If we run out of meat, we can buy some beef…We get 6 to 9 eggs a day. They are not a very good price for this time of year…

Hoping to see or hear from you soon.

Lovingly, Mary

The following is the February 12, 1913, letter from Mary to Samantha:

Dear Mother and Father and all:

Will write a few lines to let you know we are as usual. Hope you are all well. Our colds are all better. Today is Earl's 12th birthday. He took his essay to school today. Florence gave me no rest until I made salad for supper last night. I thought she would hurt herself eating it…

One of our hens wanted to set. But I guess I've got her out of the notion now. I made some nests for them yesterday. The rats are awful bad. I'm afraid they will take the eggs if I set any. Or take the chickens. We don't get so many eggs now. I only got 7 yesterday…

Earl says Frank and Josephine don't come to school now. I don't know whether they are sick or what the trouble. It is awful cold today seems to me…Old Tiger is missing today. I don't know whether he is gone for good or just visiting. Florence made a collar out of red goods Rosa gave her. She takes it off when she goes outdoors…

There has only been two agents here so far today. Write and come down when you can.

Lovingly, Mary

After the Letters

Rosa Campbell, Florence Clark, Wilmer McAdams, and Mary Clark, 1916

Regardless of what binds us—physical illness,
mental struggles, impending death—the
Lord will free us from all our pain.
—paraphrase of Psalm 107:13–14

Mary and Lester were back in their newly renovated home in the summer of 1914. Airplanes, invented by the Dayton bicycle builders Orville and Wilber Wright, were flying mail and cargo between cities. The railroads transported goods, commodities, and people everywhere around the country. Telephones were fairly common. World War I started with the slaying of Archduke Franz Ferdinand and his wife, Sophie.

Lester was busy with his livestock, crops, and politics. Wilmer was tiring of the daily grind of the farm yet continued on. Henry Ford's new assembly line increased the time of production and lowered the costs of the automobile, and most middle-class families were able to afford one. Wilmer owned a Ford Model A, and Lester drove a luxurious Maxwell Touring car.

Samantha McAdams did not feel well over the summer. Rosa had moved in with Will and Samantha for two reasons: to assist with the care of Samantha and house duties and because of her divorce from Isaac Campbell.

As the summer waned, Samantha continued on a downward health trend. No elixir, tonic, or pill could help. Wilmer, Rosa, and Mary were by her side when she died of heart failure at home on October 4, 1914.

Samantha Draper McAdams

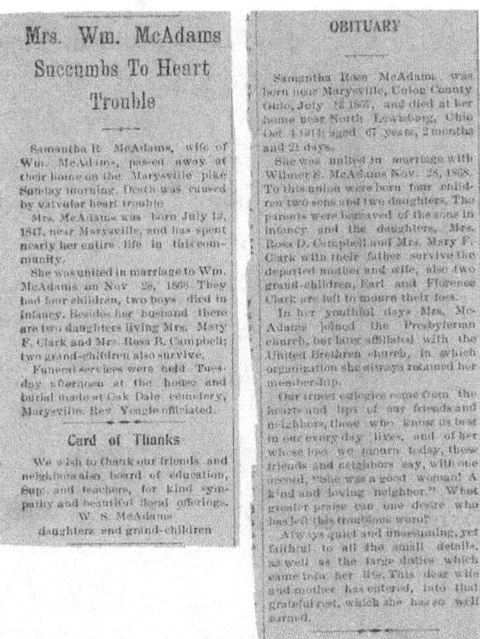

Isaac Campbell's years of severe headaches were changing the man he had been when he met Rosa. He became incorrigible and at times violent. The flamboyant trader and farmer made several unscrupulous deals that lost money due to inattention and spontaneity. Rosa took over the finances, trying to save them both from total destruction. During the summer of 1913, she had given up. By fall they were divorced.

For two years a near-destitute Isaac spent his time around the depots talking to anyone who would listen and riding trains to pass the time. The *Marysville Tribune* reported the following on November 18, 1915:

Insane Man Arrested
Unfortunate North Lewisburg Man in Hospital
Was Found in Richwood
Wanted to Entertain Urbana Deputy Sheriff at Marysville Hotel

Urbana, Ohio, Nov. 16.—Isaac N. Campbell, aged 65 of North Lewisburg, was arrested in the Erie station in Richwood late Monday afternoon by Sheriff C. E. Faulkner and Deputy John Seigle. "I'm your huckleberry," Campbell said when the sheriff told him he had a warrant for him. Returning through Marysville in an automobile, Campbell wanted to stop and treat the sheriff and deputy to a good supper at the hotel there. Later, coming into Urbana on Scioto Street, Campbell spied the name of a hotel on a sign and he wanted the sheriff to have a supper "at his expense." "Charley Faulkner has a good supper waiting for you," was Seigle's explanation, and Campbell willingly accepted the sheriff's hospitality. It was an hour after the big iron doors had closed behind him that Campbell asked one of the other prisoners what sort of place he was in. He didn't like the style of the steel-barred cells. When he was told he was in jail Campbell swore loudly and with vigor. "He asked me in to supper, and now look what he's done," he shouted.

Campbell was found in the Erie station at Richwood waiting for a train. He had two grips with him containing his wearing apparel. His overcoat was missing and he didn't know where it was. He was waiting to take a train, but he didn't know which way it was going. In fact, he didn't care. For some time, it had been his custom to board the first train that came along at North Lewisburg, going either to Urbana, or to Richwood or Marion, as the case might be.

During his younger days, Mr. Campbell had been a shrewd trader and now that his mind had become deranged, he was still trading in his imagination. He told Sheriff Faulkner he had made deals for ten carloads of hogs in the past few days. He wanted to know what sort of deal the sheriff had on in Richwood, and he was immensely pleased upon being told the deal had been highly successful. He was strong on "deals."

Sheriff Faulkner and Deputy Seigle made the trip in an automobile, going first to North Lewisburg and then to Richwood. The affidavit had been sworn to by H. V. Loder, detective for the Erie railroad, who had watched Campbell for some time and had decided to put a stop to his odd doings on the Erie trains and in the stations.

The *Marysville Tribune* covered Isaac's troubles again in a November 19, 1915, article.

Pitiable Condition of Demented Man
Thought He'd See Dick Curl
Isaac N. Campbell Expected
to Find North Lewisburg
Man in Columbus

Urbana, November 19—Isaac N. Campbell, the north Lewisburg man adjudged insane by Judge G. P. Seibert Tuesday, was gotten to the asylum safely Tuesday afternoon by Deputy Sheriff John Seigle and George Koehle. Campbell thought Seigle, when he bought the tickets for Columbus at the Pennsylvania station here was Dick Curl, a North Lewisburg friend.

"Where did Dick go?" Campbell asked Seigle when he came back with the tickets. "Oh, he went on ahead and will meet you at the hospital." Seigle explained. At the asylum which Campbell thought was a sanatorium where he would stay awhile, he was taken in charge by an attendant and taken to his quarters "to see Dick Curl."

Campbell was not violent on the way to Columbus, as the officials feared he might be. Deputy Seigle humored him along and bought almost every farm along the route at any old price, as fast as Campbell offered them for sale. Campbell was firm in his belief that he had not been in the county jail the night previous but had been in North Lewisburg, where he had made deals for 600 acres of land, had bought 17 horses and nine carloads of hogs. He was strong on deals and he found Deputy Seigle one of the best buyers on record. "I'm fed up on deals," declares Deputy Seigle. "I'll bet people on the train thought I was crazier than Campbell was."

Isaac Campbell of North Lewisburg died on July 9, 1916, at the Putnam County Infirmary in Ottawa, Ohio. The infirmary was home to those who were unable to support themselves due to illness, insanity, disability, and poverty. Rosa paid for his body to be shipped to Grenola, Kansas, for burial.

The Death of Mary

Mary Florence Clark

*And God shall wipe away all tears from their
eyes; and there shall be no more death, neither
sorrow, nor crying, neither shall there be any more
pain: for the former things are passed away.*
—Revelations 21:4 (King James Version)

During the summer of 1918, Mary was not feeling well. Florence had noticed the passing trains full of troops going by the house on their way east were less frequent. The deadly summer had taken the lives of fifty million people during the worldwide pandemic as they succumbed to *la grippe*, the Spanish flu. The disease was coming from the East Coast with returning soldiers from the war. By late September the flu had also afflicted 5,686 troops and killed 1,777 while they trained at Camp Sherman near Chillicothe, Ohio.

Everyone had been pitching in for the war. All sugar, meat, butter, cheese, and grains had been rationed. Community "victory gardens" and canning were encouraged so food could be sent to the Allies.

(Images from Ohio History Central)

Mary's cousin, George Leffler, had been killed in battle at Champagne-Ardenne, France. A letter from his sister, Myrtle Fawn, addressed to her Uncle Wilmer brought forth the horrendous news to the family.

Maysville Ohio
Sept–11–18
Dear Uncle Will.
Just a few lines
to let you know
that we read very
sad news yesterday.
Word came that Roy
was dead. He was
wounded the 28th
of July and died
two days later
in a hospital. It
surely is a sad thing
to have our dear boys
go so far away from
home and die. From
all reports most of our
Co E. boys are either
dead or wounded
or missing. Mama is
just about crazy. I
dont know what will
become of her. Hoping
to hear from you soon
Mrs Will Favor

Mary had not felt well for a quite a while and after examinations ended up at the closest major health care facility, Grant Hospital in Columbus, on August 10 with abdominal pains. An X-ray revealed a blockage of the colon. The doctor wanted to operate.

Grant Hospital required payment in advance for services, and Mary was concerned about costs. She decided to delay the operation with hope that she would get better.

In a letter to Lester, Mary requested the money that would allow her to stay. She went into detail on a clothing request for what was to become a monthlong visit. She stated that when she was not hungry, Rosa would be able to eat her fifty-cent meal.

An August 12 letter from Mary to Lester read:

Dear Lester,

From what I heard I don't think they are sure what is the cause. There is an obstruction but they could not determine the cause. I would rather take treatment for a while and see. If I could see you, I could talk lots better. If there is an operation, I couldn't come home for 18 days after.

I expect the operation would be a few hundred dollars. So, it would be cheaper for me to stay a few weeks to take treatment. Then if I should take worse and the operation had to be, I will be here…It makes me sick to sit up…How terrible it did jolt coming down here. I think it was good for me. Along with the treatment they gave my bowels yesterday eve, they begin to act very little. So, I rested a little better last night. I expect I will have to ask you for another check for $50…As soon as I can get out of bed Rosa will come home. I know she is needed there…Hope you are all O.K. and getting along good. You had better ask Pa to come over to eat sometimes. Answer soon.

Lovingly, Mary

Lester and Mary could afford the required care and hired a private day nurse, Anna Barlow. Rosa would stay with Mary during the tribulation, attending to Mary when nurse Barlow was not on duty.

In an August 13 letter to Mary, Lester wrote:

Dear Mary,

Just received your welcome letter. Good to hear from you. That you was feeling well. But you did not no what was coming. Glad you braced up so brave. I heard about it last eve that you was alright. Hope you are still feeling better. I will send you a check for $70.00. I received a statement that the ex-ray examination was $20.00. So, you can settle that and take receipt for it. Will have to close.

With love, Lester.

Letters of news were sent from Earl and Florence, reassuring their mother that life was moving along but that they missed her. Rosa often wrote return letters for Mary when Mary did not feel well enough to write.

An August 13 letter from seventeen-year-old Earl to Mary read:

Dear Mama:

How are you today? Is it hot down there? I haven't been doing much lately. Say, when is Aunt Rosa coming home? It is almost a case of "root hog or die" with us. Clara Holycross came over yesterday and baked some pies and cookies and cooked a chicken and some potatoes. The chicken is about gone also one pie is missing in action…

Lovingly, Earl Clark

"Root hog or die" was an expression that came from the practice of turning pigs loose in the woods to fend for themselves. It meant that you must look out for yourself because no one is going to do it for you.

On August 13 twelve-year-old Florence also wrote to Mary:

Dear Mama:

How are you feeling? I am feeling fine. Don't worry about us…Zip [the pet dog] misses you. Mrs. Weatherby and Papa are jabbing away. Ha ha. Yesterday when we got home, she was out in the yard in a little wooded chair knitting. She lit the coal oil stove at noon to get dinner. I saw the coal oil was getting low so I told her it was getting low so after a bit she turned it out. I thought you wouldn't want her to use it. This lady is too lazy for everything. There hasn't been any troop trains going through…The lady gets mad at Zip sometimes. Last night when we went out on our ride, we took Zip. Earl went back to Grandpa's. He stays at Grandpa's at night. He comes over in the forenoon. I am glad you have good nurses and doctors. Aunt Rosa staying there too ain't she? If she reads this letter tell her you will read it yourself. If she asks why tell her I said so. Tell her I didn't write it for her to read…If I can get down there can I come home with you in the ambulance?…

Good bye, Florence

Mary had the necessary operation on August 14. Rosa wrote the following letter from the hospital to Earl and Florence:

Dear Earl and Florence:

I have been back to the hospital about half an hour…The Dr. says mama is getting along as well as could be expected. She says for you to be sure and take your baths and put on clean clothes on Saturday…The water here is as clean as crystal. There is a scarcity. The government has taken control and they can't get all the ice they want here…

Yours lovingly, Aunt Rosa

Rosa wrote again on August 15 from the hospital to Earl and Florence:

Dear Earl and Florence:

The nurse says mama's condition is better in every way…Mama wants you to be sure and clean your teeth. And she says if you need to use the coal oil stove for Mrs. Weatherby to take the tank off and fill it and then use it if you need it. She wants you to keep account of the eggs you sell, what they bring and how many and account of the cream…There are several North Lewisburg people here. Mrs. Frank Cornell is here with Mrs. John Thompson. Mrs. Doug Louden is here. The Dr. brought Nellie Spain down the other day to a rest hospital. We see Dr. Freese 3 or 4 times a day. There are 28 babies on the third floor. We can hear them cry sometimes. Florence the nurse thinks you hadn't better come down for a while yet. She wants mama to keep as quiet as possible. Earl, I expect that chicken and pie that Clara cooked looked and tasted good. Are you catching any fish? I want to get home for a day or two before long anyway.

Lovingly, Aunt Rosa

In one letter exchange, Mary requested a visit from Lester. She had been in the hospital fourteen days, and Lester had yet to visit her. On August 24 Lester wrote Mary a letter expressing concern over expenses of the hospital stay. He also said he could drop off the children for a visit while he visited the State Fair in Columbus. This, of course disappointed Mary, and she sent a quick-cutting retort two days later.

Mary:

Received your letter yesterday just after I saw Dr. Finsterwald. He told me just about the same as you did. How you was about [the same as] the first I had heard…You had $170.00 the day I was there in the bank. I will send $60.00 makes $230.00 all told. You must be careful and know what becomes of the money. If you can't keep track of it, I will have to come down every once in a while to see after it. You say you will send word when to send the children down. I may come down to the Fair. They could come then and I could go to the fair till they was ready to come home…

by by, Lester

Dear Lester:

I am not able to write, Rosa is writing this for me. I just finished reading your letter. Yesterday was the first day I have been able to know myself…I have wondered why you and Earl didn't write to me. I thought as sick as I was you might have written. There is something wrong about the money. There isn't as much as you think there should be, but by going after them yesterday evening we found there was more than we thought. As for sending the children over, I don't remember of anything being said about you sending them. I expected you all to come. Be sure and have the machine [car] fixed in good shape because school will be here before long and if it was fixed you could come over every week or so. I think you all ought to come over and do trading for school one day this week. Mary has gotten sleepy and tired. So I will close. It will be all right for you all to come over one day this week. Good bye.

From Mary by Rosa

The length of the hospital stay was wearing on everyone. Earl and Florence were running out of suitable clothing, and everyone missed Mary being home, especially with the new school year coming up.

An August 27 letter from Florence to Mary read:

Dear Mama:

How are you feeling tonight? I am alright only I have a couple of splinters under my fingernail. Lois [Stetson] is playing the Victrola…Joe Overfield is going to Tennessee on a taxi. He gets $125.00 a month. He was to start today but grandpa said he was fixing his machine. Lois is dancing the one step. She was dancing a while ago and I told her it was through and she stopped and stood there awhile and looked at it then commenced dancing again. Grandpa got two Gordon tires for his machine. I could tell you lots more if I could talk to you…When we come down, I am going to get you lots of ice cream. Did you mean for us to do our trading at Columbus or Marysville? How much money shall I give Earl when he wants money…Where are Earl's everyday shirts, his new ones? Has he gotten anymore underclothes besides the pair he is wearing now? I saw one in the sideboard. It is tore to pieces now…Good bye. Write when <u>you</u> can. With heaps of love and loads to the one I love best.

Note that twelve-year-old Florence was asking about giving money to her seventeen-year-old brother when he wanted it.

On August 27 Rosa also wrote to Lester, Earl, and Florence:

Dear ones at home:

Mama wants me to write and tell you that she wants Papa and both you children to come down this week and grandpa too if he can come…Florence, mama says she has a new gauze shirt wrapped in paper on the second shelf in the downstairs closet and a corset cover hanging in the corner in the downstairs closet. She wishes you would bring them when you come down…

Thanks for the pressed flowers, Aunt Rosa

An August 28th letter from Florence to Mary read:

Dear Mama:

How are you tonight? I was glad you sent a colored picture of the Hospital…When I come down, I am going to get you ice cream. And kill one of my young Banty's. And fry it or [prepare it] anyway to suit you…The Dr. asked papa when he was going to see you…We are coming down tomorrow. Then going to the fair for a while…Monday school commences…Papa and Lois was telling each other what fortunetellers told them. Papa's [said,] "you will have to keep a tight hold on your pocket book for everybody imposes on you." Lois's said, "your man is going away and get killed. I feel sorry for you."…Oh dear the blots, grandpa said he is not coming down tomorrow. For one of them would have to stay and turn the cows over to water…

Good bye Florence. I love you little, I love you big, I love you like a little pig. Some love small, some love large. I love <u>you</u> best of all.

Grant Hospital, Columbus, Ohio

An August 29 letter that Rosa sent to Lester, Earl, and Florence read:

Dear ones at home:

Rec'd Florence and Earl's letters this morning and was glad to hear from you…Mama doesn't feel so well today. She didn't rest well last night. We were expecting you all over today or tomorrow. Mama wants you to do your trading over here and you better do it while I am here. Earl have you sent your shoes back? Mama says you can have $10 out of the milk money…Florence you can use what you need out of the egg money. Earl get the oldest milk checks cashed what you need to get your money… Florence, Mama says for you to play the piece that you like best at the recital…Earl hasn't any underclothes besides the ones he is wearing. If they are gone, he will have some new ones. If your tires haven't come yet why can't you drive grandpa's machine to Milford and come over on the train. Mama wants to see you…Lester, we looked for you down at the fair. Mama says she doesn't want you to play the Victrola too much so as to wear it out. Earl, I am glad you like your position as cook. I expect grandpa is getting fat on it. Mama appreciates the pressed flowers Florence. Your Mama still has her nurse. They thought she had better stay awhile longer…Mama sends lots of love and so do I, Aunt Rosa.

The children were excited for Mary to come home on September 7. While Mary was still in the hospital, Florence sent an invitation to her for a welcome home party on September 11, 1918.

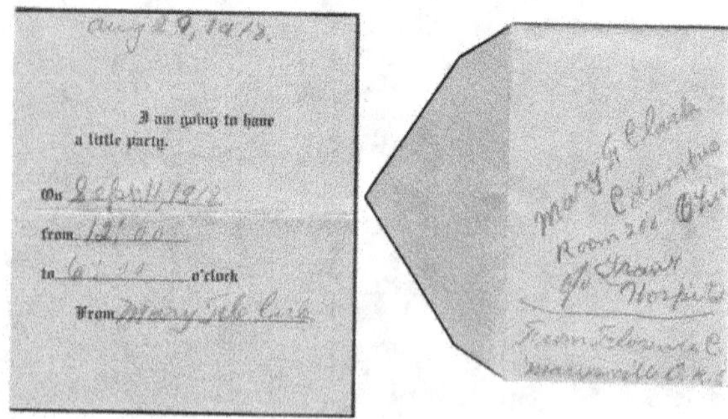

A September 5 letter from Rosa to Mary read:

Dear Sister Mary,

I called Dr. Finsterwald this morning. They told me you're getting along alright when they left…The roads are bad. We had plenty of rain yesterday and it is cold. It is bad weather for the fair. Grandpa and Earl have gone…I don't suppose I will write again as you wouldn't get my letter before starting home Saturday. Hoping to see you and Miss Boyle soon.

I remain your loving sister, Rosa Campbell.

To the relief of all, Mary came home. The children, Lester, Rosa, and Grandpa Will were all ready to get back into the routine of daily living.

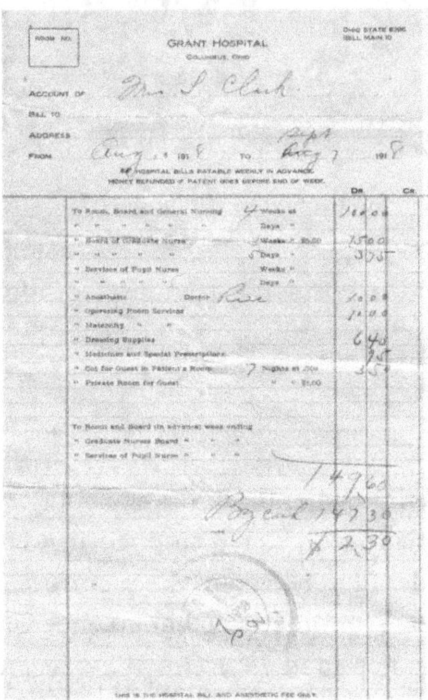

Grant Hospital bill for Mary's thirty-nine-day stay. Dr. Finsterwald and nurse Anna Boyle were additional expenses.

The ongoing pandemic, the war rationing, and Mary's operation made for a miserable summer. The Spanish flu had taken such a toll on lives that on October 10, Ohio governor James Cox and his team met to write and release "Instructions to Local Health Officers for the Prevention and Control of Influenza," highly suggesting that public gathering places, schools, non-essential businesses, and saloons close. The good news in a horrible year for the world was that Germany signed the Armistice at Compiegne, France, ending World War I on November 11.

Face masks were a common sight in 1918 (photo from Alamy)

Mary was back in the hospital by January 20, 1919. A January 21 letter from Rosa to Mary read:

Dear Sister:

I hope you are feeling better. I got home about 2:30. The Dr. had a little trouble with his machine. We stopped in Marysville. Had to wait about an hour…I let Florence go to the picture show with Earl. I didn't think you would care for me letting her go once without me…I thought maybe it would do her good…Give my best regards to Miss Wells and with oceans of love to you I remain your loving sister.

Rosa

A January 22 letter from Earl to Mary read:

Dear Mama:

How are you? Maude and Teddy [the horses] came all right. Zip won't let the cat in the yard. I got through my examination yesterday…I got forty in algebra and eighty in history. I think my English and physical geography grades will be about like my history grade. We surely got it soaked to us in algebra. The highest grade was eighty and the lowest was zero with a lot of fives and eights. Florence and I went to the picture show last night. It was "Come Through." It was the best one I have seen up here for some time. I can't think of anymore. So, I will close.

Yours with love, Earl C.

Actress Alice Lake played Velma Gay in the silent picture *Come Through*

(photo from Wikipedia)

A January 22 letter from Florence to Mary read:

Dearest Mama:

How are you tonight? I hope you can sleep good. I slept till six or half past. Gladys Watkins asked me if I could go to her house to stay all night. I don't care if you say no for I don't want to go very bad. I went to the picture show last night. My but it was good. The title was "Coming Through"…[nine handwritten pages of movie description]…Good bye. Don't forget to write when you can.

Lovingly, Florence Clark to Dearest Mama

A January 23 letter from Rosa to Mary read:

Dearest Sister,

I rec'd Miss Wells's letter and was glad to hear from you and that you were resting comfortably…I have been trying to get the house cleaned up. Mrs. Bishop, Mrs. Beltz and Mrs. Thompson called up this morning and inquired about you…I think Florence must be like you. She can write such a good letter. She is practicing her music and studying her lessons. She is a regular woman about some things well. I must close for tonight. Hoping this finds you better.

I remain your loving sister, Rosa

Doctor examinations revealed that there was nothing more they could do to help Mary. She was sent home to North Lewisburg. Mary's nurse, Anna Boyle, composed a touching letter on January 31:

My Dear Mrs. Clark:

May God give you His blessing—patience to endure all and comfort and love. That's what counts in this life anyhow…I do want you to do all that you can to try to get well. Keep a stiff upper lip. That helps. Do not see the hole in the doughnut but look for the doughnut…May God bless you and give you strength to do His will in all things. With love to all.

Anna Boyle

At age 39, Mary died on March 1, 1919, at the home of her father and sister.

Mary Florence Clark, September 11, 1875, to March 1, 1919

The memorial card passed out at Mary's funeral offered comfort with the following poem:

> A precious one from us is gone.
> A voice we loved is stilled:
> A place is vacant in our home,
> Which can be never filled.
> God in His wisdom has recalled,
> The boon his love had given,
> And though the body slumbers here,
> The soul is safe in Heaven.

After Mary

Lester, Earl, and Florence Clark with cousin Frank Edson at Brush Lake

Even though we have been hurt, we must find a
way to get through it, life goes on whether we want
it to or not. The world keeps turning no matter
how bad we feel. This is why we have to learn how
to bounce back and keep moving forward.
—Rashida Rowe

Mary's death left the family floundering. Lester continued to pour all of his attention into farming and assisting his father-in-law, Wilmer, on his farm. Rosa had been living with her then seventy-two-year-old father since her divorce from Ike.

Earl and Florence continued with their schoolwork after moving in with their grandfather Will and aunt Rosa. Earl was always close to his grandfather, and Florence was very fond of Aunt Rosa. Between the farms, livestock, trading, and politics, Lester just did not have time for the teenagers. Earl was easygoing, loved the outdoors and machinery, and played football. Florence continued to excel in her studies and music.

Earl in front of North Lewisburg High School (left) and Florence (right) in 1920

Earl graduated from high school in June 1921 at the age of twenty. Academic work was not his forte; he was hands-on. Earl was intrigued with the mechanics of the Victrola when he was younger. He ignored the grime under his fingernails while tinkering with farm implements and the workings of the automobile. He made an early crystal set to listen to faraway radio stations. Earl could hunt, fish, and trap with the best of them. He was also ready to continue his destiny as a fourth-generation Allen Township farmer.

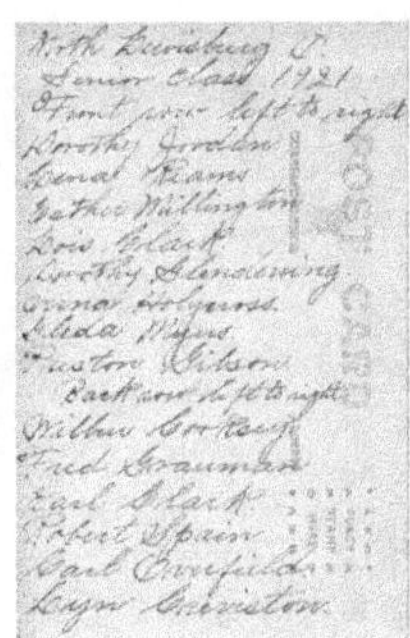

North Lewisburg class of 1921. Earl Clark is in the back row, third from the left.

One month after Earl's high school graduation, Lester tripped and cut his hand on a sharp piece of metal while crossing the tracks that ran through his property. He contracted blood poisoning from the laceration. On July 10, two years after Mary's death, Lester died at age seventy-four.

GOOD CITIZEN DIED ON TENTH OF JULY

LESTER CLARK, OF ALLEN TOWNSHIP, PASSED AWAY IN GRANT HOSPITAL.

The editor of the Journal regretted very much to learn last week upon returning from his vacation, of the passing of a good friend and citizen, Lester Clark of Allen township, and also to note that the Journal reporter had overlooked mention of this fact. Mr. Clark died in Grant hospital, July 10. Some days previously, in crossing the Erie tracks which run through his farm, he stumbled and fell, scratching an arm on an old piece of iron. Blood poisoning set in. He went to the Fountain Park sanitarium for treatment and later was taken to Grant hospital in the ambulance of Floyd Freeman of North Lewisburg. The day before his death he underwent an operation but the poisoning had progressed to such an extent that death ensued the day following.

He was born on the old Clark homestead, February 17, 1847, two and a half miles east of North Lewisburg, in Allen township, and was a son of Caleb and Rachael Beltz Clark, his age being 74 years, 4 months and 23 days. There were nine children in the family and Lester was the last to pass away.

On October 13, 1870 he was married of Jerusha Poling. They were the parents of one child, Hattie M. Carmean. After her death he was again married, to Mary McAdams, September 5, 1896. They had two children, Earl and Florence Clark. The second wife died March 1, 1919.

Mr. Clark was a member of the Methodist church in Marysville. The funeral services were held Tuesday, July 12, at two o'clock at the residence of Don Carmean in Marysville, with Rev. J. A. Hoffman in charge. The interment was in Oakdale cemetery.

Lester Clark with one of his prize horses (left) and Earl, Wilmer, and Florence (right)

President Warren G. Harding, from Marion, Ohio, had won the presidency with women voting for the first time after the passage of the Nineteenth Amendment. Harding declared peace with Germany, Hungary, and Austria. World War I was officially over. Earl and Florence had just lost two parents in two years and didn't care about world news. Wilmer and Rosa had many problems to solve. What would they do with the farms? The farms were a big operation, and Earl's interest wasn't totally immersed in farm life yet. Florence, a budding musician at fifteen years of age, played the piano and violin.

Wilmer McAdams on his porch

There were crops in the fields that needed to be harvested in the fall. The horses, cattle, pigs, and chickens needed attention multiple times each day. Day laborers needed to be hired to tend to the animals. North Lewisburg was a kind community, and when called, men and women were there to help with dinners and the immediate labor. Earl and Wilmer did their best to continue the operations while Rosa and Florence cooked, cleaned, tended the chickens, made butter, and canned vegetables.

The effort was too much for Wilmer McAdams. Four months after Lester died, on October 30, 1921, a tired and spent Wilmer McAdams walked to the barn, threw a rope over the rafter, and stepped off a milking stool. He was seventy-two years old.

Wilmer McAdams

Rosa Campbell was now head of the family. She became the legal guardian of Florence. Earl continued to assist with the two farms as Rosa worked to sell the assets.

Below is the value of Lester's estate as recorded in the *Marysville Journal-Tribune*:

The estate value property value is over $45,000.00.
North Lewisburg property, $500.00.

Allen Township farm of 135 acres, $16,875.00.
Middleburg farm of 95 acres, $5,700.00.
West Mansfield farm of 125 acres, $11,295.00.
Other Logan County acreage, 10 acres.
Equipment and livestock, $6,364.00.

Lester's son-in-law, Donald Carmean, was the estate executor. He charged the estate $8,204.08 for his services. The amount seemed excessive to Rosa, and she sued the estate for $1,287.00 to cover the cost of boarding Earl and Florence for two years.

The perceived inequity and Rosa's action angered Hattie, and she sued Earl and Florence to force the sale of the farms. Within a year the estate was divided unevenly between Hattie, Florence, and Earl. Hattie received the larger portion of the estate, and Florence received a fair portion and, for an unknown reason, Earl the lesser.

In the spring of 1922, Earl met Marguerite Gilliland of Urbana. Peg, as she was known, and her brother Jack were raised by their father, William Gilliland, and stepsister Charlotte Walter. Their mother died when Peg was six years old.

William Gilliland was a baker and businessman. He bought small-town failing bakeries. He would reenergize the business, sell it for a profit, and move on to the next opportunity. At the turn of the century, grocery entrepreneur Bernard Kroger of Cincinnati, Ohio, expanded his store from one to four. His desire was to continue to expand and to add bakeries to his stores. Kroger sought out William Gilliland for advice and offered him a partnership. William didn't want to work in the big city and said no thank you to Kroger's offer and continued on his way. Peg rarely spent more than three years in any one town as the family moved several times throughout Ohio and Michigan.

Earl and Marguerite married on August 6, 1922, after a short courtship. They moved to Hartford, Michigan, where Peg's father was updating yet another bakery. Earl worked as a real estate agent. That was not a good occupation for Earl.

Jack and Marguerite Gilliland, 1917

Earl Clark, 1927

During the 1920s people became more prosperous from the restocking of America after World War I. Everyone was entertained by radios. Most homes had telephones. The flappers were going strong, dancing the Charleston. With his trumpet, Louis Armstrong was adding a new variation to music called jazz. In 1927 *The Jazz Singer*, starring Al Jolson, became the first "talking picture." Charles Lindberg made his heroic nonstop flight from New York to Paris.

After a short stint as a real estate salesman, Earl moved with Peg to Grand Rapids to be a policeman. It didn't take long for him to decide that he was not cut out to be a policeman; it was not in his personality. Four years later he was working at what he truly enjoyed.

As the Depression engulfed the country, Earl found his calling as a union electrician and welder. He was never out of work the rest of his life. However, he did move on to the next opportunity. His first electrician job was with Consumers Power, stringing wire on poles. Over his career, Earl and Peg moved to eighteen Michigan communities as he found electrical or welding work.

The Clarks had a daughter, Carolyn, and a son, Jim. The most time the family spent in any one place was five years, during which both Carolyn and Jim graduated from Comstock Park High School. Carolyn went on to a nursing career, and Jim held positions in the federal government in Washington, DC. Carolyn had four children with her high school sweetheart, Wally Matthews. Jim Clark remained a single man until his death.

Earl and Florence Clark, 1958 (left), and Earl and
Marguerite "Peg" Gilliland Clark, 1960 (right)

Earl died of a heart attack on September 12, 1961, at the age of sixty while he was at work remodeling the Lansing, Michigan, post office. Marguerite died at age seventy-three from cancer in 1977.

Florence Rose Clark went on to excel in school after Mary's death. She practiced the piano and violin daily, with Aunt Rosa's encouragement. After her high school graduation in 1925, Capital University Conservatory of Music in Columbus accepted Florence as she furthered her music vocation.

North Lewisburg class of 1925. Florence Clark is front row, center.

The Epworth League of North Lewisburg, about 1927. Rosa Clark is on the left. Florence's cousin Jenny Clark, second from right, made a very generous donation to the Marysville Hospital upon her death.

Florence was a fastidious person. The diary she left of the years 1925 through 1929 provides a very comprehensive account of her life. After her Capital University experiences, Florence taught piano, was active with the Epworth League, and played piano at church and the "picture shows." She lived with Aunt Rosa on Maple Street in North Lewisburg.

Florence Clark, 1925

The roaring twenties were great times, as the country transformed from a rural base to an industrial giant. The style of clothing changed, as did the lifestyles of the day. Elegance was a fashionable "boyish" shape that minimized curves. The invention of a diminished brassiere made of silk and lace replaced the heavy fabric of Victorian brassieres and cumbersome corsets. Lighter and less apparel was worn. Skirt levels rose from the ankle to just below the knee.

Florence had plenty of suitors. North Lewisburg's finest courted her—Hugh Notestein, Elmer Huber, Carrol Poling, Wilber Sauers, LaVonne Curl, Max Coates, Pearl Cline, and Worley Dooley—only to be rebuffed. Worley did not give up as easily as the others, as he continued the conquest. There was mutual interest. But there was also competition, a free-spending man and the postmaster of North Lewisburg, Lester Overfield.

Overfield's personality and background were similar to that of Isaac Campbell and Lester Clark: older, experienced, and dominant. He had been married, his wife had died, he had a young son, and he was thirteen years Florence's senior.

Lester's age concerned Florence, and she was hesitant to date him. She finely gave in to the charming conversationalist. He bought Florence candy and presents and was there every day to take her places in his new car. Soon they were the darlings of the town. They would sing together in the Methodist Episcopal Church choir and the Epworth League. They had a quartet that entertained at many social functions with Paul Spain and Clark Buchwalter.

> **QUARTET SINGS**
> The quartet of North Lewisburg, under the direction of Miss Florence Clark, composed of Earl Burroughs, first tenor; Paul Spain, second tenor; Clark Buchwalter, first bass, and Lester Overfield, second bass, sang the selection. "Wayside Cross" at the M. E. Conference, held at Urbana. Their music was among the most favored numbers of the evening entertainment.

The unknown newspaper music review, circa 1926, was found inserted in Florence's diary.

Florence and Lester dated for two years. She enjoyed her life as the local music teacher, and she and Lester commanded a lot of local attention. Lester kept wooing young Florence. Select entries from her diary follow:

August 31, 1927
Lester came down in the evening to show me new auto. Took ride. I drove part way. Nice.

September 3, 1927
Went to Russel's Point in p.m. Took boat ride, aero plane ride and a railroad ride.

September 18, 1927
Lester came down late in the evening…I wanted to go to the picture show at Marysville, "Romona." Good. Loving. Left at 12:30. Kind, loving like lovers in picture show.

Lester and Florence were engaged in February 1928. He wanted to buy a farm with her inheritance. His overbearing persistence bothered her. Florence was concerned that he liked her for her money.

March 30, 1929
Gave piano lessons in the morning. Went to Urbana with Lester and folks, also Aunt Rosa. Didn't expect to bid on the farm when auction started. Lester bid for us. Sold for $58.50/acre. $6800. 116 acres. We got it. [Paid for with Florence's money.] Played for picture show. *Thanks for the buggy ride.* Lester took me. Loving.

April 30, 1929
Took dinner out to farm

May 1, 1929
Got home 12:00. Talked seriously—we don't agree on money. He thinks I should buy new tractor and plows, that is, put my name on note with

his. Afraid too much for first year and pay for farm. Thinks I should put up money for other things. I think he asks too much. Loving—more so at last. Makes me feel that he doesn't exactly want me as a wife.

On May 15, 1929, Lester and Florence had a huge disagreement about money:

He got quite angry and said he would rather be disappointed now than after marriage. I told him that I was purely crushed.

May 15, 1929
Talked. Said he loved me and nothing must happen now to prevent our marriage.

On June 29, 1929, they exchanged vows.

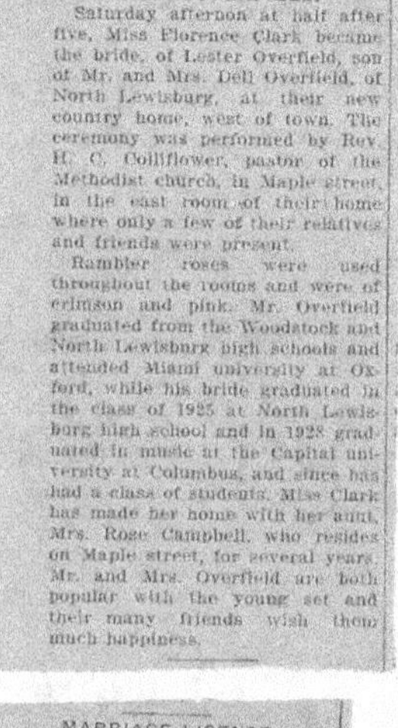
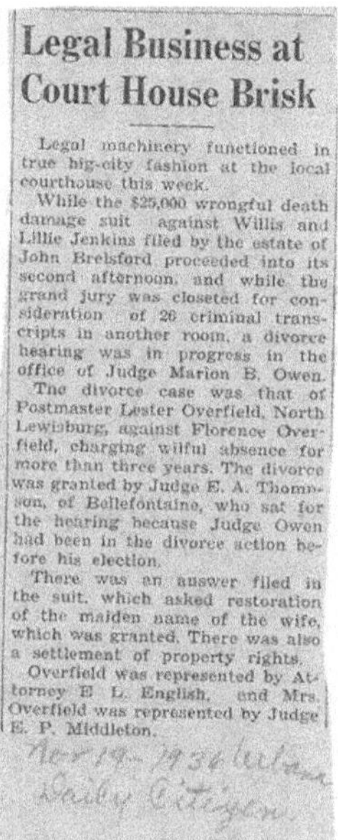

CLARK-OVERFIELD.

Saturday afternoon at half after five, Miss Florence Clark became the bride of Lester Overfield, son of Mr. and Mrs. Dell Overfield, of North Lewisburg, at their new country home, west of town. The ceremony was performed by Rev. H. C. Colliflower, pastor of the Methodist church, in Maple street, in the east room of their home where only a few of their relatives and friends were present.

Rambler roses were used throughout the rooms and were of crimson and pink. Mr. Overfield graduated from the Woodstock and North Lewisburg high schools and attended Miami university at Oxford, while his bride graduated in the class of 1925 at North Lewisburg high school and in 1928 graduated in music at the Capital university at Columbus, and since has had a class of students. Miss Clark has made her home with her aunt, Mrs. Rose Campbell, who resides on Maple street, for several years. Mr. and Mrs. Overfield are both popular with the young set and their many friends wish them much happiness.

MARRIAGE LICENSE

A marriage license has been issued to Lester D. Overfield, 34, farmer of North Lewisburg, and Florence R. Clark, 25, music teacher of North Lewisburg.

Legal Business at Court House Brisk

Legal machinery functioned in true big-city fashion at the local courthouse this week.

While the $25,000 wrongful death damage suit against Willis and Lillie Jenkins filed by the estate of John Brelsford proceeded into its second afternoon, and while the grand jury was closeted for consideration of 26 criminal transcripts in another room, a divorce hearing was in progress in the office of Judge Marion B. Owen.

The divorce case was that of Postmaster Lester Overfield, North Lewisburg, against Florence Overfield, charging wilful absence for more than three years. The divorce was granted by Judge E. A. Thompson, of Bellefontaine, who sat for the hearing because Judge Owen had been in the divorce action before his election.

There was an answer filed in the suit, which asked restoration of the maiden name of the wife, which was granted. There was also a settlement of property rights.

Overfield was represented by Attorney E. L. English, and Mrs. Overfield was represented by Judge E. P. Middleton.

Lester Overfield and Florence Clark

Unfortunately, the marriage didn't work. Two years later, Florence left the farm to Lester and went to live with Aunt Rosa in her Maple Street home.

Rosa Campbell and her home at the corner of Maple
and Linn Street in North Lewisburg, Ohio

Aunt Rosa Campbell died of a heart attack on October 28, 1936. Lester's divorce for Florence's willful absence of more than three years was granted twenty days later, November 18, 1936.

Florence soon moved to Springfield and worked as a secretary at Wright Patterson Air Force Base until her retirement, never to marry again. Florence died on August 15, 1977.

The Allen Township farms provided good lives for three generations of McAdamses and Clarks for one hundred years. The men originally worked the land with an ax and horse-drawn plow. Later, families worked with gas-powered machines. Though the women's "separate sphere" of daily life was not as revealing during the century, the women were forever hardworking, and their irreplaceable accomplishments were many.